Eternally, Yours Faithfully

Roy Radford & Evelyn Gregory

Illustrated by Lin Bourne

Eternally, Yours Faithfully

©2000 Roy Radford & Evelyn Gregory

ISBN 186163 1049

Cover design by Paul Mason
Cover and internal illustrations by Lin Bourne

Published by:

Capall Bann Publishing
Freshfields
Chieveley
Berks
RG20 8TF

Acknowledgements

We express our appreciation for the help given to us during our work on this book by Ray Branch, Bert Gregory, Elizabeth Hampton and her friends at the 'Little Valley' sanctuary, to Debbie Lewis, Ursula Radford, our many new-found friends world-wide and, especially, we gratefully acknowledge Sue Parslow, and Jacquie Wright whose guidance and assistance, respectively, has been invaluable.

Dedication

We dedicate our book to past friends and companions Charles, Cheryl, Evelyn, Francis, Grace, Mollie, Patricia, Terri, Calico, Puddy, Pussacat Willum, Sooty, Sparky, Thee, Tinkerbell, Tiny Wee, Tippi, and Tramp. Each, in their own way, has been instrumental in convincing us that an open mind helps to make clear the way ahead.

Roy Radford & Evelyn Gregory

Contents

Chapter 1

A Pet in Passing or an Angel in Disguise?

As we walk our dogs, come home to our cats, feed the gerbil, rabbit, or other family pet, does it ever occur to us that if 'Angels' walk this world of ours, it is certain that they appear in many, friendly, forms? In our close encounters of a furred kind, are we surrounded by 'friends' who daily attempt to reveal to us the true meaning of devotion, trust, and eternal love, while we, in our ignorance, fail to even recognise that we are in the presence of Angels ?

These 'Angels' we refer to care nothing for status, high or low, for any worldly rank we humans might attain, or the privileges we enjoy but, the closer to us we permit them to come, the more readily they recognise when ill befalls us, and seem always ready and prepared to share the troubles the world can inflict upon us. They feed upon love, share the warmth of friendship, comfort the lonely, and ask little in return.

Those 'angels' closest to the hearts of people are most easily observed when recognised as their companions; a person's beloved pet.

Other creatures, untamed, might draw near more warily, but regularly, to share some kitchen table crumbs perhaps, cast upon the ground, or nuts provided in the worst of weathers, or yet a feast brought forth by the turn of a gardener's spade.

There is no need to seek Angels, for they will find you; embodied in the plainest of guises. They have no need of shining wings, or mysteries. That small brown bird; a stray ginger cat; a dog, a robin redbreast; a flower that has grown where none was planted. A trapped honeybee, waiting to be righted and set on its way, with love, not fear. A hungry hedgehog; a lone urban fox who stops in his tracks and looks at passing traffic; the tree that provides shade for you on a hot day, and shelter on a wet one; these are a few of the Angels.

Some, we suggest, are here to guide us, all are here to help us, and then there are those that have passed on from this place and who return to show us the way ahead.

To gain understanding it is necessary to look --- and really see, to listen --- and really hear, to be silent---- and allow the wisdom in your heart be heard.These words have inspired our work but, in reality, can our eyes ever be open enough to help us recognise Angels ?

We have been fortunate in sharing with many people from many countries their thoughts, and experiences of the bonds that they built with animals in their homes and workplaces, and the pleasures they gained from working with or caring for them. We were left in no doubt about their wide ranging views, and the beliefs they hold about their animals and pet/companions. Coming together with a pet/companion is not a matter of chance or sheer luck for anyone who then finds there is purpose in companionship; and some purposes extend beyond life itself.

We now consider ourselves fortunate to be able to regard all of these people as our friends and, as friends do, we talked openly with each other as we shared our experiences.

As our circle of friendships widened, the talking, and communication by letter, fax, or e-mail, all helped the sharing and, more importantly we now recognise, it led to a us all sharing experiences we might otherwise have kept to ourselves.

There were so many avenues to explore, so many viewpoints to consider; and learn to consider with open minds. When one friend raised a question, another invariably had the experience to answer it. We believe that nothing happens by accident.

The encounters we personally experienced had brought us contact with many other that had similar experiences, and far more in addition.

We were all travelling the same road, but we soon learned that in one way or another, we could each make the journey a little easier for another by listening, sharing, learning, and caring.

Holly and Mistletoe are two Caribbean cats we came to know, through JMW.

'Our two little angels, Holly and Mistletoe, joined our family on December 21st 1996 but the story of how they came to live with us started a few weeks before that.

We live on Grand Cayman, which is a small island in the Caribbean. There are lots of insects, lizards and frogs here, so our house has screens fitted at all the windows and doors so that they can be left open without things flying or crawling in.

One evening we heard a rustling in our front room and went in there to see a large fluffy ginger cat looking very much at home.

He was very friendly and looked well cared for, but didn't have a collar or a name tag. Wondering how he had got into the house we checked every window and every door, and found all the screens intact.

He didn't seem in a hurry to leave and followed us around the house while we tried to see how he had got in. It seemed impossible that he had walked through the open door with us as surely we'd have seen him but there was no other way he could have got in.

After feeding him some tuna we sent him off, hoping he'd find his own way home.

Late that night I did wonder if it was the spirit of my Gran come to say goodbye to me on her way out of this world. She loves cats and I'm sure she won't leave without saying goodbye, so a visit in the form of a cat seemed a good possibility.

A phone call the next morning disproved that theory though as she was alive and well, and wished she'd seen the ginger cat. Thinking no more of it, a few weeks later a friend mentioned that a friend of hers was fostering some cats that were due to be sent over the Rainbow Bridge, as they'd been in the animal shelter for some time and had not been adopted.

4

We had been thinking of getting a cat but, selfishly, kept deciding it would be too difficult to deal with when we went away: and any other excuse we could come up with. To appease our friend we agreed to call around and visit the cats, but didn't think we'd be able to help. Two hours later, with a borrowed litter pan, litter, food dishes, food and some cat toys, we were carrying the little angels home. They were so friendly. Both had immediately come over to us, purring and meowing, and they were so pretty (one was handsome, as we later found out) we couldn't leave them to their fate.

We let them explore the house, following slowly behind and the first place they went to was the spot where we'd found the ginger cat. It may be because they could smell his scent but I like to think he'd been their guardian angel looking for a home for them and had found us. To this day we've never seen the ginger cat again but Holly and Mistletoe have brought so much fun and pleasure to our lives, we're very grateful he chose our home for them to live in.

A year later when discussing cats at a dinner party, it turned out that my husband's new employer was the original owner of our cats. He'd had to pass them on when they started a family and moved to an apartment where pets were not allowed. We were very pleased to be given some of their kitten pictures so now we don't have to say "we bet you were beautiful kittens", we know.

From what we know of Holly and Mistletoe, neither of them are ginger, so they seem to have had a friend, rather than a relation, who was looking after their interests J.B., of Gloucestershire, was one for whom the giving rather than the receiving of a cat provided her with an unusual experience, which she was pleased to share with us."

"Some years ago we took in a little all black stray cat who, it turned out, was expecting kittens. She duly delivered 4 black ones and 1 beautiful all grey one. I had lots of interest in the kittens, but everyone wanted the grey one. In the end three people were all begging me to let them have it, and I had to choose the one who I thought would make the most suitable owner.

I gave him to a friend I had known for a long time, and she took him home delighted. About eight weeks later I suddenly awoke in the night and looked towards the clock on the bedside table, and I couldn't believe my eyes, even in the darkness I could see a kitten sitting on my bedside cabinet looking at me. I blinked my eyes, but he was still there, I reached out my hand and he just vanished.

The next day, the husband of the friend who had the grey kitten, came round very distressed and said that the evening before, he had been putting his car away, checking carefully that the kitten was on the lawn chasing moths, but as he reversed into his garage he felt a bump and he had run the poor mite over and killed him !"

Despite her misgivings when she looked at the clock on awakening, J.B was sufficiently sure of what she was looking at to put out her hand to touch the kitten. At the time she was not even aware that there had been an accident involving the favoured grey, so there was no reason for her to 'imagine' its nocturnal appearance. There was certainly nothing imaginary about the poor mite's unfortunate death so, why did the kitten return ?

JB was the one who had lovingly taken so much care over finding it the right home, she would soon hear of the accident but, before that news reached her, the kitten appears, seemingly to inform her of its passing, and of its progress. JB is in no doubt that what she saw was the ghost, or spirit, of the kitten.

A few years ago a dachshund dog owned by F.D., of Hull, was accidentally killed.

"At the time this happened, my mother was on holiday but I didn't go with her. I stayed at my brother's instead. Unfortunately, because my brother had a cat that Bess was afraid of, she remained at my sister's instead. Anyway, I visited Bess every day.

However, on the Tuesday after seeing Bess and making my way back to my brother's home, I had a strong urge to go back and see her. I dismissed that urge as I said to myself I'll be seeing her tomorrow. That night my sister rang, and said that Bess had been run over and killed. Apparently the back gate had been left unlocked and that's how she got out. My sister became worried about Bess after she had been calling her and she hadn't returned. As you can imagine I was very upset and felt very 'empty'.

It was two days later, on the Thursday, that my mother returned from holiday and I went back home from my brother's. That night I dreamt I came downstairs and saw Bess on her favourite rocking chair, which she used as a bed. She said to me through mind to mind communication "I'm all right." And that was it. You may say that because I dreamt this, it wasn't real, but I can assure you that it was real. She came to comfort me by telling me she was fine now. But, I strongly believe her death was fate. Because a few weeks before she died, I had an impulse to take lots of photos of her and also that strong feeling on the day she died, as if I should see her one last time. There was, however, more than one close encounter that F.D., had experienced and her earlier experience was such that it demonstrates that personal contact with, or knowledge of, an animal is not required for an encounter to take place.

"My mother also had a dog in her early teenage years called Jess. She was a cross-breed. Well, when I saw her, I wasn't dreaming. It was during the day and I was awake and this experience happened before Bess had died. Anyway, I was stood in the lounge and I just happened to look down and I saw this dog standing next to me. All of her body wasn't clear: I just more or less spotted her back (this view didn't seem strange at the time either). I noticed she had a dark line down her back. When I told my mother what I'd seen she said that Jess had a strip down her back where her hair parted.

F.D., believes it to be a fact that her mother had never previously discussed her childhood pet with her, nor that she had heard the dog described by anyone else, yet she could hardly have been more accurate in describing the dog herself, a dog that she had never encountered; in life that is.

"I simply saw my mother's pet dog from her child-hood days," she wrote. She did also add that there had never been any photographs of the dog in the house which she might have come across, and remembered.

"No photographs, no memories of descriptions, no nothing. I simply saw Jess beside me for the first time. I hope this proves to some people that there is 'life' after 'death'. I'm most certainly a believer. There's a lot more which exists that we can't comprehend yet" There certainly is, but it doesn't require a pet to be deceased before we can recognise that close encounters come in many ways, and to serve many purposes.

One such encounter happened when J.C., from Devon, arrived at a cattery to seek out a cat to share her home. What she was looking for, she was fortunate enough to find and she later called her new friend 'Poppy.' Like many others who have written of their own experiences, JC has much to say about the cat she found that needed a home, and about Poppy's progress and well-being since she brought her home; until seven words give rise to other considerations.

"Poppy settled down extremely easily and seems more than happy in her new home. She is a very affectionate, lovely cat who adores human company, and is a constant source of pleasure to me. She is my constant shadow, "supervising" my life, and apart from her brief sorties into the garden, she likes to be involved in whatever I am doing.

After living for some time with a very old cat who seldom made a sudden move, initially, life with Poppy was like living with a very small, very fast moving, bulldozer, although she now seems settled and is slightly less likely to plough her way through precious ornaments! And she has finally decided that walking on the carpet poses no threat to her delicate feet, after spending the first few months avoiding doing this at all costs (which gave some of my furniture a pretty hard time)!

When I took her home I knew nothing of her background, not even her age, but it seems that she was not much more than 12 - 18 months old, as she still had so many kittenish ways. She is developing nicely into an adult cat, has gained weight well, and now has to be curbed from her somewhat greedy tendencies.

She is an insatiable thief where food is concerned, and unattended food anywhere, including other people's houses, is fair game to her "hunter's" instinct ! I am more than delighted with my adopted lodger !!

I have had an emotionally tough year, and Poppy has added so much pleasure to my life (even though I can't quite appreciate her early morning "alarm call" of wailing, leaping from one side of the bed to the other across my head, and chewing my feet !). Poppy 'chose' me when I visited the shelter, and I hope that if she could talk she would say her choice was the right one !"

This fortunate cat obviously landed on all four paws by being in the right place at the right time when JC called at the shelter but, for us, there is a niggling little doubt that Poppy is only a lucky lodger. Many people would say that Poppy was 'fortunate,' and that is all there is to it, until, perhaps, just seven words that JC wrote are considered again;

"I have had an emotionally tough year."

JC, we realise, had needs herself, and she goes on to confirm that she too has benefited enormously from this partnership, with the words, "Poppy has added so much pleasure to my life."

As the last line of her story reveals, JC recognises that she became a 'chosen one,' yet she seems also to infer that the reason for Poppy choosing her, was because she could provide a good home for the cat. But isn't there, possibly, a little more to this than meets the eye ? Poppy needed a home and needed help; JC had a home, and also needed help. The place that Poppy found wasn't just 'lodgings' it has every appearance of being a home 'intended' for sharing.

As we shall show, there are many ways in which close encounters satisfy more than one need. With JC's adoption of Poppy we suggest that the needs of both the cat and the person were satisfied but, can that be attributed just to 'luck'

When Elizabeth Hampton provided us with her thought provoking poem. *"Surplus To Requirements,"* she also drew our attention to the story of two dogs, named Florrie and Kizzie.

Surplus To Requirements
Why am I here ? What did I do ?
How could they walk away ?
Perhaps they're coming back for me,
Tomorrow; - or today ?

My hopes are slowly fading,
'Til I realise, for sure,
That I'm surplus to requirements
Not wanted any more !

In so few words the continuing plight of the unwanted, abused, and ill-treated dog or cat is revealed; even if it has been fortunate enough to find safety, kindness, refuge, and regular food all provided in an animal sanctuary. With the older dog or cat in mind, Elizabeth's words read and re-read are likely to strike a chord in the conscience of anyone who has sought and rescued a young cat or dog, but in doing so walked on past the older souls.

How easily her words could be applied to an older human too, as she sounds her warning of the loneliness and despair. Doesn't how we treat our animals reflect how we treat each other ?

There is every reason, however, to recognise that loneliness and despair can be felt at any age; by any animal. There is also every reason to consider that we, as individuals, may be called upon, or guided, to do something about these problems.

It might seem that we can either choose to help when called upon, or ignore a situation since humans generally consider their role in this world as one of 'being in control.'

Should it then be beyond consideration that we are often chosen, and regularly picked for a purpose. The picking, the choosing, and the purpose can all be considered in an item which, if we were putting headings to thought provoking pieces within a chapter, for this one we might select; "There's A Place For Us."

A black and white terrier cross, aged about three, was seen emaciated and starving and scavenging through rubbish bags in the street to find food but, by good fortune or fate, the sad plight of this weakened outcast was recognised by someone who cared.

Florrie, as she became known, was taken to an RSPCA animal rescue centre, to recovery, and towards a new and fulfilling life. Some years later, any specific discussion on whether Florrie would have survived, or indeed could have survived, without the help that the animal sanctuary provided is certain to have been resolved with a definite conclusion; 'No.'

We go beyond this, however, and suggest that Florrie's rescue and recovery is worthy of another consideration, specifically; that it was 'intended' she should survive.

A week after Florrie first learned that food could come from friendly hands, and to the total surprise of the sanctuary staff, the weakened girl gave birth to seven healthy puppies. The first 'intended' reason for Florrie's survival must be seen as one that provided her with the opportunity to give life to the litter of pups she had somehow managed to nourish within her own emaciated body. Briefly, they were hers in a triumph of motherhood over malnutrition and abuse, Mother Nature's intention overcoming human ignominy. Then they were gone and Florrie rested her weakened body.

She did indeed survive for her puppies, bringing them to a place where they would be born in safety, where they could be fed and cared for, then offered a future; but there were other reasons too. While her offspring thrived in their new, safe, world Florrie started out a journey through new experiences where she encountered and understood friendship for, perhaps, the first time; and learned the heartache of rejection.

Unlike the people who brought her food and water and talked to her every day, there were others who came to the sanctuary. Strangers, smiling strangers perhaps, but strangers nevertheless. People came by whom Florrie could not immediately trust, so she cowered away as they sauntered past her kennel; their interest was not in her, anyway. There were little bundles of life nearby, playing their puppy games, chasing, tumbling, jumping for the joy of living. These yapping youngsters, whose voices Florrie could recognise, was the attraction the visitors took more notice of; but gradually they diminished. Not the visitors, they still came.

The voices diminished as the puppy family grew less in number as one by one they were carried away by smiling strangers. One by one as they left, Florrie associated their departure with a parting playful puppy yelp, a smiling human face, and shoes; all kinds of shoes. Shiny patent leather shoes, brown brogues, boots that were made for walking, silent treading trainers, sober suedes; and, once, a pair of yellow wellingtons.

When the last of her family was taken from the sanctuary Florrie only saw shoes - walking away. She had long since stopped wondering whether a face would smile on her, the way she had seen them smile on her puppies. Now there was not even the sound of puppies distantly playing, and Florrie was alone again. The staff who comforted her with caring hands, could hardly make her raise her head. A friendly voice encouraged her to, "come for a walk," and she went; but the grey of the road, reflected in her downcast eyes, expressed her mood. The voice was that of a friend indeed.

The walks became regular excursions; the companionship appreciated. Roads began to appear less grey, the verges somewhere to explore, and walks became something to look forward to. Visitors still came to the sanctuary, some even glanced her way at times; but usually only in passing. Occasionally a visitor would actually stop by Florrie's kennel, their faces smiling just at her, but when they turned to talk with staff, their impatient shoes never smiled. Always the shoes walked away again, leaving behind them a loneliness that Florrie felt with every passing day, as keenly as any biting wind.

The people looking after her were there, every day. Now familiar friendly folk, with kind faces and comforting hands, encouraging her to overcome her frustrations. She demonstrated her affection by coming close, with a wagging tail showed them she valued their friendship, then watched their shoes walk away. Florrie was alone again, until another 'friend' came along to take her for a walk.

For the next ten months Florrie settled into a routine in life, and in that routine was this one recurring factor that was to have a bearing upon her future.

Monica was looking for a dog, not just any dog, but one that would get on with others she had. She visited the RSPCA animal rescue centre and looked all through the kennel block. As an experienced dog owner she knew what she was looking for, but couldn't find it. Not one dog in the whole place suited her requirements. For Florrie, there was to be no happy ending to her story that day.

For some reason, which the staff could not understand, visitors seeking a dog to share their home with always passed Florrie by. She was becoming a long-term resident of the Centre; one who knew the routine; one who enjoyed the regular walks she was taken for by the sanctuary's staff or voluntary helpers. Life was far better now than when she had been starving in the streets, but what of the future ?

Monica was still looking for a dog, and she didn't give up. A week after her first visit she returned to take another look around the kennel block; and this time she found Florrie. Despite Monica's thorough search a week earlier, this was her first encounter with Florrie, for good reason, as we can learn from her;

"The previous week she had been out on a walk, so I did not see her."

The simple routine into which Florrie had settled, had almost let her down; but not quite;

"The staff seemed somewhat surprised that I had chosen Florrie. She had been with them a long time, and continually passed over by prospective owners, for no known reason.

The sanctuary Manageress told Monica that she believed Florrie would make a loyal and loving pet but, at the outset, life with Florrie was to prove very difficult and to be full of problems for her full-time human companion.

"At first life with Florrie wasn't easy. She did not want her lead to be put on. and flew at me twice. She was dirty in the house for a while, and hated being left on her own, even for two minutes while I went upstairs. She also barked all the time while I took her out, at whoever we met, even if they didn't have a dog. I started to build up her confidence and although it has taken a long time she is now a very clean dog and much happier and relaxed."

Monica was recalling those incidents some three years after having taken Florrie into her home and while she was recounting events in the lives of Florrie and another of her rescued dogs, Kizzie. Once an unwanted Lurcher, Kizzie had been dumped in the Blue Cross kennels when she was ten years old, but now, with loyalty and affection, she demonstrated daily how grateful she was for Monica having rescued her. Now she added her own welcome to the once unwanted Florrie.

The doggy duo certainly got on well with each other and for Monica, a registered nurse, this provided interesting opportunities. Her canine companions, she decided, could participate with her in a the nationally promoted 'Take Your Dog To Work Day,' one Friday in June.

Owners were being encouraged to support the day and celebrate the centenary of the Blue Cross organisation, the rescuers of her very own Kizzie, to help raise money for the Blue Cross building fund, and to promote the presence of dogs in the workplace. Most would consider these reasons sufficient to give the event the support called for, but Monica had yet another reason to join in. As a nurse who specialised in the care of the elderly she knew that it was becoming ever more widely recognised by those in the medical profession that dogs help to reduce stress, lower the blood pressure and provide a source of interest for the elderly.

It is of particular relevance to our story that it should be noted that this was not going to be a first time that Florrie and Kizzie had accompanied Monica to work. They had gone with her at times when she worked in a nursing home and the patients had loved it. Florrie had even been hospital visiting, and taken her own particular brand of pleasure-giving along with her. On this occasion, the dogs were to dress the part and Monica purchased a special Blue Cross bandanna and dog-tag for Kizzie to wear, since she was a Blue Cross dog after all, and for Florrie she obtained a doll's nurse's cap that fitted perfectly. Thus prepared, nurse Monica set off to visit her patient accompanied by her two canine companions and when they arrived at the patient's house;

"Florrie's first job was to clean the carpet of any crumbs while Kizzie did her rounds in the kitchen and brought me a packet of cat food she found on the floor. Florrie watched me make the bed and told me with one 'woof' that the postman had called, while Kizzie did some light gardening. Both dogs met my patient and she was very interested in them. Florrie demonstrated her agility talents by jumping over the Zimmer frame (fortunately with a clear round). My patient was certainly entertained by the dogs and took several photographs....."

The day was a great success and that work experience inspired Monica to enter Florrie and Kizzie in a national competition. Placed second, some might think they only came close to winning, but how wrong they'd be. Both dogs were once unwanted, abandoned, and unable to trust any human. Yet both came to be valued as companions by Monica, and brought joy to elderly people. Florrie has also achieved a great deal in Obedience, Agility, Dog Shows and the Kennel Club Good Citizen Scheme.

Was it really just by chance that Monica visited the Blue Cross kennels when the abandoned Kizzie most needed someone to find her?

Was it just coincidence that Monica returned to the animal rescue centre for a second time so soon after finding only disappointment there on her first visit? That Florrie would become a loyal and loving pet proved to be an accurate prophecy made by the sanctuary Manageress. She and her staff, plus the volunteers who helped at the sanctuary, all played their part in ensuring that Florrie survived; and the Blue Cross kennels people helped Kizzie.

Can it be disregarded that Monica's profession provided, not one, but two dogs with the means and opportunity to help others? Was this all co-incidental, and should we simply believe that it all came about, by chance? Or should we consider more fully the possibility that it was 'intended' that Florrie should indeed survive? And Kizzie also, for that matter. In telling her tale of two dogs Monica added that she did so;

"...to encourage owners to keep their rescued dog, even if at first they have problems and have contemplated returning the dog to the centre after 2 weeks. It can take quite a time, plus patience and perseverance, to successfully re-home some dogs with a background of cruelty or neglect."

Those are sentiments we endorse, patience and love can work wonders but, on this occasion, did rescuers, sanctuary and kennel staff, voluntary helpers, a nurse and two dogs, all respond to a powerful Spirit that simply said, 'there's a place for us'?

Ossie

I have dog called Ossie,
Whose start in life was poor
I got him from the RSPCA
When they opened up their door.

He dines just like a king,
And lives just like a lord
But he is mine, and we just seem
To have struck a loving chord.

The love I have for Ossie
Is more than I can show
He follows me at every step
Wherever I may go

He is a constant shadow,
But he never is a bore,
And he is now so full of
  life,
What did I do before?

Margaret Kernoghan

Chapter 2

Who Are, More Often Than Not, The Ones Chosen?

Many people will consider that their needs are satisfied when they find, or rescue a pet but, the needs of our pets are satisfied far more often than many people appreciate when the selection of a companion is made; and the pet is, seemingly, the one that chooses the companion.

For anyone who considers him or herself not to be an animal person or whose lifestyle is not one that allows them to provide the care, attention, and companionship a pet-person relationship should include, the realization that a pet has chosen them can come as a shock.

For busy people, career seekers, or simply the socially active, the desire to enjoy the companionship of a pet sometimes overlooks the fact that the pet might need companionship more often than the person can provide it.

In any community there will undoubtedly be those of whom it said, "they shouldn't be allowed to keep that cat/dog, not with them being away from morning till night." Even when the owner is ever present, similar sentiments regarding the keeping of a pet will also be heard when the poor creature in question is considered to be in need of TLC, and regular food also, perhaps. The personal experience of working in the entertainment world from early morning until long after midnight, with rarely a day off, let alone a holiday, is an experience considered to have been a privilege but it definitely excluded any possibility of establishing a pet-person relationship.

In that time consuming world of pop groups and orchestras, concert artistes and comedians, civic ceremonial and royal personalities, the prospect of keeping a pet could not even be considered. Even returning to rural roots didn't alter things. My wife, Ursula, and I, followed the removal van into the village in which we now live one wet and windy October day and found a warm welcome from folk who were ready to lend a hand to get furniture into place and show us how to get the fire going in the old cooking stove. We didn't have the heart to tell them we'd both spent our childhood cleaning, clearing and lighting even more ancient stoves but we did have to admit that we didn't have any pets when the question arose. Plans we had a plenty, animals we had none; as yet.

Ducks and geese were among the plans, since there was land enough with the cottage for us to look forward in anticipation to eggs galore, come the spring perhaps.

A month later, our work took us away from our new home to present two major craft fayres, one in Portsmouth Guildhall and the other, later, in Wilton House, the home of the Earl of Pembroke. By the end of November we were back in Devon planning the following year's content for the annual Hampshire County Show, which we had created, funded, and then presented in the superb riverside setting of Netley Abbey, near Southampton, with the co-operation of the County Council.

As we were working one evening we heard someone knocking at the cottage door, and it certainly didn't enter our minds that it was a visitor who was going to alter our lives. Ursula responded to the tap, tap, tapping and was somewhat taken aback when she opened the door and faced a furry creature being thrust towards her. From the shadows two ladies stepped forward as Ursula stepped back into the cottage. The cat seemed unconcerned and an explanation for its presence was immediately forthcoming.

"His owner's died and he hasn't got a home," said one of the kindly visitors framed in the doorway.

"You haven't got any animals, so we thought you might look after him," said the other, adding, "Here's a tin of Kitekat."

The cat disregarded the tin of food being waved above its head and was content to be carried into the cottage by its bearer as the two ladies stepped forward. Not being a fully paid-up 'cat' person, I chose to take the Kitekat, which left Ursula to deal with the furry visitor. The ladies, one still cuddling the cat, settled into two fireside chairs and began to relate the tale of how the cat had been 'orphaned.'

Perhaps it was the warmth from the log fire that did it but the cat began to purr as we heard how the villagers had ensured that, after learning of its owner's death, it had been fed regularly. After the funeral the villagers had decided that the cat could not be left to go wild, and that suitable long-term accommodation should be secured on its behalf.

The 'newcomers' in the thatched cottage, who had no animals, were the obvious, and apparently unanimous, choice as potential adopters. So that was that, really.

Our visitors were comfortable in their chairs, the cat was sleeping peacefully and, strangely somehow, neither of us could find any argument to raise against our selection. The imitation we were giving of goldfish out of water, as our jaws silently opened and closed, was taken as wordless expression of our overwhelming pleasure at having been given the seal of approval. Advising us, cordially, that the villagers, "will be keeping an eye on you," the ladies took their leave, the cat took up residence on the arm of one of our chairs, and our lives changed.

If, then, we had been regarded as a gullible couple, villagers will only now be learning that their decision to offload responsibility for a homeless cat was one that brought us more joy in the subsequent years than we could possibly ever have imagined possible. However, we did not get off to a start that included immediate acceptance of us by the furry boarder. Only a couple of hours after accepting responsibility for the cat I was stretched out flat on the wet road outside the cottage trying to coax it from its place of refuge beneath a parked car, by torchlight.

Trying to see eye to eye through Devon drizzle with an apparently discontented cat, in an attempt to convince it of our good intentions, remains an indelible memory. Yet, despite a memorable soaking, I 'know' those waterlogged moments cemented our friendship. With Ursula hovering nearby, reminding me that the eyes of the village could be upon us, I coaxed the black and white feline out from beneath the wheels and into our lives; thankfully.

In the dark of night, it was indeed a testing time but not, I believe, for the cat. The test was for me. I later became convinced that 'Puddy' was helping me to decide, there and then, whether my independent spirit would get along with his. Having made the effort he expressed his own o p i n i o n clearly b y

ambling out from beneath the protection of the car, leading Ursula swiftly back to the cottage, and leaving me lying on the soaking wet road. I picked myself up, and followed them into 'our' house. If he didn't select us to provide him with a home, we don't know who did.

Together, the three of us shared many years of companionship. We had our ducks and geese along the way, with Puddy's approval obviously. He was quite prepared to let the little ones, hardly out of their eggshells, to stay beside him and when Puddy was on guard they were undoubtedly safe from any airborne attackers. He stayed with us for many years. During his lifetime with us we learned a great deal about pet-person relationships, and after he'd gone we found, like many others, that the learning didn't end.

G H told us that:

"as a child I had a tabby cat called Tig who died of natural causes at the age of twelve or so. I had always been fond of him but Tig, like most cats, had his own life and I suspect my affection was unrequited. We buried him in the garden. Within a few weeks we had a visitor - a large tabby who could easily have been one of Tig's descendants as his colouring was so similar. The curious thing was that he would sit on Tig's grave, in the way that cats just sit, doing nothing much. He was obviously owned by somebody as he was fully-grown and a good size for a cat, but my mother began feeding him. (She's mad about cats and probably missed Tig.)

Eventually he came to live with us. He was quite different temperamentally from Tig, mainly because he had been neutered by his previous owners. It made him a stay-at-home cat. He was a very nice pet and I grew very fond of him, enjoying seeing him stretched out in front of the fire, covering nearly all of the fireside rug. (He was big.)

The only problem was that he didn't like our other two cats. Nor did he like the four young children who visited us regularly (neighbours from the same street). One day while these children were in the house, I could tell he had had enough by the look of disgust on his face. That day he left and never came back."

G H was obviously disappointed at the departure of her friend, but even in this parting, which didn't involve death, was there not perhaps a lesson learned? The adult G H, writing of a childhood memory, clearly remembered that her friend had not liked other cats, and certainly didn't like children. When they were present she could recall that, "I could tell he had had enough by the look of disgust on his face."

The cat that came after Tig chose only to visit, not to stay, yet during that brief encounter left a lasting reminder in G H's memory that a home is, after all, a place first and foremost for the people who choose to live in it. A rather lighthearted reason for a pet to 'move on' was also remembered by GH who said that we,

"may be amused that a friend of mine who met this cat (whose name was Moggy) told me he thought the cat looked like Lee Marvin. I could see what he meant: it was the rugged features. You'll remember that Lee Marvin sang the song about being born under a wandering star. Moggy obviously took this comparison seriously. Perhaps even made it to Hollywood."

Now, we know of dogs, chimps, and mules all making it big on the cinema screen so, perhaps there's a musical Moggy yet to come.

Just as humans expand their circle of friends or acquaintances, by choice, and in doing so also extend their experiences, wherever people expand their circle of pet friends, there are often similarly extended experiences. A group of, say, four humans may develop and demonstrate friendships and loyalties that are based upon the concern they have for each other, as chosen companions throughout their lifetimes. Where pet-person companionship and choice is concerned, the experiences of many people indicate that those friendships and loyalties are just as clearly recognised and demonstrated between the pet and the person. D G of Lincs., recognised and experienced this oh-so-valued relationship;

"Two years ago, I had to have my lovely little girl Jessie put to sleep. She was a black/white puss of around 14. I had her for ten years, she was a stray, which chose me. She had a tumour on her mouth and nothing could be done,. The tablets kept it at bay for 8 months, but we knew when the end was near, I rang the vets, it was around 10.30pm, before I took her. I told her that I was sorry that I couldn't get her better and thanked her for all the love she had given me over the years. I was crying and said 'please come back Jess and tell me that God is looking after you please. Don't forget me as I love you so much.

I brought her back from the vets and laid her down, on the rug in front of the fire, to show the other cats so they would know. Monty licked and washed her and he and Puddeth and Pip stayed with her all night,. The next morning I dug a grave and said Goodbye. The other three cats looking out of the window.

All day, I was so upset, during the evening, Monty all of a sudden started to call out, the other two were up in my bedroom, he ran across the room and acted as if something was there. I could see or hear nothing. I fussed him as I knew he was missing Jessie, they were very close friends. I went to bed. Monty came with me, he came inside the bed, I could not sleep still being so upset, when I felt something jumped on the bed. I put the light on, to see if it was Pip, as Puddeth always stays downstairs, there was nothing there !

I put the light off and then felt something walking up me, I stayed still and shouted. Jessie is that you? I felt her come to my face and purr, Monty came out of the bed to see her and talked to her, she stayed a very long time. I put my arm round her and could feel the weight of a cat. She did this, for two nights, the second night she licked my face before she walked down the bed and then the weight went, and she never came back again, but even though I could not see her, only feel her, Monty saw her and even now Monty looks strange, odd times, as if he can see what I can no longer feel and I'll say, is it Jessie, and he purrs.

That is a true story, I was not afraid, she came back to tell me God was looking after her."

The continuity of her relationship with Jessie, experienced by D G of Lincs., was confirmed not by another human who might have wished to pander to her emotions, or her emotional state, but by Monty who had previously shared his own friendship with Jessie, as well as with D G. The common factor of close-shared friendship among humans is readily recognised, and no one would ever really consider it relevant to note or question the number of humans involved that may share the experience of the loss of a friend from among their group. It is natural, and it is not noticed.

When the friendship factor involves both people and pets in the group, it is no less natural, but when the shared experience continues for one pet and one person, it is more noticeable when they each recognize the loss of the mutual friend, and they both recognize the return, or the presence of the same friend; at the same time. The knowledge of the return, or the presence, of the friend by both pet and person increases the potential for understanding.

D G, in fact, was able to draw our attention to another experience that had taken place some six years earlier. In order of content in her letter, however, this was to her the 'second' experience she wished to draw to our attention. It is an experience we were sorely tempted to put into first place, in accordance with the time difference between the two. That was until we reached the editing stage. Then we realized that there was much to learn from the order in which the message had arrived from D G.

"I had a stray, three-legged black cat, called Poppy, again, she choose me. Arrived in a heavy snow storm, the fact she had 3 legs did not seem to bother, her getting around, but she did get spasms on it and I had to massage gently the stump every day. After 3 wonderful years together she got ill, not too ill, but lost weight, after a blood test, the vet said she had kidney trouble, but she could live quite happy with a tablet twice a day, ' it's only a mild kidney inf-ection and it was not life threatening' so I brought her back from the vets with this large bottle of tablets. She refused to take even one.

I put her in her basket in front of the fire, she licked my hand, purred, talked to me, then just laid still. I did not know what she was doing. I kept trying to get some more response from her, but nothing. I tried to give her a tablet, no way. She would not move. I rang the vets, he said play some soft music, stay with her as she is depressed now, at being ill, but I'd got to encourage her. So, I stayed, by her side, for 3 days / nights.

I was angry, very angry, at Poppy and God, here was a lovely cat, who is packing up the will to live because she feels unwell and can have treatment to live. I asked God (I am a Christian) to help Poppy. I kept saying over and over again, 'I hate you God, because you are not helping Poppy. Give her the will to live, take her out of her depression', but no.

The last night, Poppy moved, she lifted her head, looked at me, purred and talked then died, she was gone my lovely 3 legged Poppy left me. I felt it such a waste, why had Poppy, wanted to go, did she not love me? During the week I went to church, and in front of the altar I said, I hate you, God, why did you let Poppy lose the will to live. I don't understand it, give me an answer.

After two weeks of being upset, hurt angry, I was not hardly eating. It was after I had just gone to bed I put the light out and lay there, upset, when all of a sudden, I felt very funny. I was being taken up off the bed, the room had gone, then in the darkness, I could make out a door. I tried to get near the door, but it would not come any nearer. I was not frightened, and spoke the words, 'why I am here?'.

Then the door came to me, I knocked on the door, for it had no handle, it's just a wooden door, no sound came. I knocked, knocked, 'let me in' I shouted, then the door opened. I went in and there in front of my eyes was Poppy, sat on a chair with 4 legs not 3. I could not believe it, she purred and I kissed her she was so happy, she talked and I held her, then from within the room a beautiful light came and a voice said, "Poppy, came because I called her. She is with me now and always in heaven, she will be here for you." and I said 'I want to stay, please let me stay, if this is heaven'.

A 'window' appeared and in the light I could see all sorts of animals playing with each other, no pain, just all love. And I said again, 'Let me stay with Poppy'. I put my cat down, back into the chair, and walked towards the light, then the voice said, "you have to go back, it's not your time, but it was Poppy's, I called her".

Then everything went, before my eyes all blackness: and I was on the bed. I put the light on and could not believe what had just happened, but it had, it was real, a message from God, to tell me, there is a heaven and animals are there. Since then, every chance I have at church, I'll tell people that in heaven, God has all his animals and they are healed, I cannot talk about people, because I did not see any in that 'window', only animals, but God came to answer my prayer because my faith had gone, for I was so cross with him, but now I am so happy for Poppy for I know she has four legs, animals are perfect, so God takes them straight to heaven, this I know.

It was not a dream. It was a real event and changed my life, that is why some animals come back to us, to tell us, there is a heaven, that's why Jessie came to say God sent me back, a short stay to say God is looking after her well."

The extra message we learned from the order of D G's letter was that only six years previously she had such little faith that she was angry with God, argued with God, fought with God and made demands of God.

When things don't go their way, don't many people do the same thing? Yet, at the end of her experiences D G knew that it was the returning animals that brought with them the understanding that most of the rest of us are seeking. If they were returning, there was definitely, 'somewhere' to come back from. Since that time she has not doubted this. Through the experience that she shared with Monty, there is no doubt expressed about the return of her friend Jessie, from 'somewhere,' only a doubt about being able to recognize a presence, as easily as her pet does.

M L H, from northern England, chose as a career to be a bereavement counsellor, for animal loss and, as might be expected, not only hears the experiences of others, but also has them of her own, as her letter regarding Pearl, and Thomas Pinkerton, will illustrate.

"I hear many stories of sight, hearing, feeling, and sensing of the lost animal, proof indeed - if any were needed - of an afterlife. I am psychically linked to cats, and to a few people.

Pearl: On two occasions I saw him around the house, and I know that he watches over what I do. When my 5 year old cat - Joe - arrived a few weeks after Pearl died - he did not behave as a kitten would to a new environment - exploring, touching, playing with everything. He just knew where everything was and accepted that this was his place to be, after a shaky start.

Pearl, I feel, was with him - had brought him here and already told him where everything was - all he needed to know - for some time - and still with some traits - he behaved like Pearl - so Pearl was with him. He looked as me with the soft eyes of ancient wisdom that had come from Pearl.

My earlier experience was when I was at college - between 1981 and 1984 certainly and I was missing the cats I had had to leave behind. I was the closest to Thomas Pinkerton - a truly intellectual cat. I felt lonely in my bed without the feline company - and there he was - rolling around on my bed for a few seconds - and I felt so much better.

I am pleased that you share my appreciation of the feline - my cats are my brothers and sisters, my children and the best of friends. All animals - of course - deserve the same respect - of the insects - dragon flies and woodlice are among my favourites. One of the things I always tell my clients - who are mostly quite spiritual - is that the love they share with the animals never dies - and it is so important to remember that."

A and M B are a couple living abroad who regularly keep in touch with friends in England whom, in turn, shared with us a story from a dog that must rate itself highly among those truly 'chosen' ones.

"Last summer I was what is known locally as a 'Barrel Dog'. This is because my home was a disused oil drum. I had none of the comforts known to many other canines; no cuddles, no kind words, toys, or even a decent meal. My staple diet was bread and olive oil, with the occasional bowl of water.

My name was 'Ella' (which is Greek for "come here"). One day whilst doing my job of guarding the chickens, whilst tethered by a length of rope attached to a circle of wire around my neck, a lady walked past me. She spoke to me in a language I didn't understand, but I took an instant liking to her. She

kept saying 'pretty girl' to me and I responded by wagging my tail and holding up my front paw to her. Her name was June, and we very soon became the best of friends.

I looked for her every day, and she brought me tasty food, tit-bits and dog biscuits.... something I had never had before. She said she wished she could take me home to live with her and spoil me - she said I was emaciated, whatever that was! Anyway, from what she told me, she already had a dog, and there was no way he'd make me welcome over his threshold; that was his domain. However, next thing I knew was that I was being untied from my rope, and the wire collar was removed and replaced by a red leather one!! I felt very important. Apparently June had found my owner and asked him if she could have me, and he agreed for a small price.

I moved in with June and have never known such luxury. I had my own chair..... my very own chair, with a duvet on it! I felt like royalty. 'Gazza,' the resident dog gave me a hard time though. He snapped and growled at me and told me to get out of his home. He didn't have a kind word to say to me; I tried to make friends with him, but he didn't want to know me. June separated us, one upstairs, the other down. But things didn't work out at all well. Gazza won the day and I had to leave.

I was taken to the Animal Shelter called "Noah's Ark", and hated it there. I spent my time planning my escape to find June, my newfound friend. I missed her, and the way she would call me 'pretty girl'. Two months passed, and I still hadn't managed to outfox the shelter's workers, and run away. But then, to my delight, I was rescued by June. She hugged me and called me 'pretty girl', and said we were going home. I wagged my tail so hard I thought it would drop off, and held up my front paw to her, - I was so pleased to see her again. How could I ever repay her for coming to get me?

Apparently Gazza had gone to doggy heaven, so I was able to move in, lock, stock, and barrel... but my barrel days were well and truly over. June fed me on chicken and steak. I had vitamins and conditioning tablets and felt 'full of beans.' I put on weight and looked and felt in the best of health. My coat was glossy, I was getting regular exercise and meals, and veterinary supervision - it was wonderful !

On December 14th 1996 I gave June a special present for all her kindness and devotion to me - 8 puppies !! She was

delighted, and said I was a clever girl. Her friends visited and chose which puppies they wanted and duly took them when they were old enough. None went to 'Barrel Homes', "only the best for our boys and girls," June said, and I definitely agreed with her. I am now settled into my new way of life with June; she runs an English tavern in a holiday resort called near Hania and her place is popular with the tourists.

June to me is enchanting, and my best friend. I love her so much I wonder if she'd like some more puppies!? Only joking."

Ella, a red setter, was renamed 'Nellie.' Two of her puppies, Penny and Tuppence, are now companions to A & M B who admit to 'spoiling them rotten'.

The 'chosen ones' choose each other with amazing regularity, as the experiences contained in the correspondence we receive from people around the world continue to show. The need for a home, the need for help, the need to share, the need for a purpose in life whether pet or person, all feature among those experiences we are privileged to hear about, and share.

Then there are those experiences which make us wonder just what might have happened if just one pet and one person had, for any reason at all, not chosen each other. For P B it is a query we are very pleased indeed did not arise. One good turn may well deserve another but, consider this;

"He was a large black and tan German Shepherd dog, with sad brown eyes, unwanted and unloved. My daughter heard about him from a friend at work, and came home in tears. He was about to be taken out into the country and abandoned somewhere that weekend. Being a dog-loving family, and despite having a dog of our own, we decided to rescue him until we could find him a good home.

Our old dog Skipper was a bit offended at first, but very quickly they became firm friends and went everywhere together. It was a joy to see his eyes gradually become bright and alert, and his tail begin to wag when we spoke to him. He had only had 'Boy' shouted at him, so we called him 'Bron' and we kept him. One day we had taken the two dogs out for their evening walk, and my husband had stopped the car outside a shop in order to buy them some treats. I was sitting with the window down, when suddenly a very inebriated man, who seemed to hold a grudge against the world came rolling along the pavement, shouting abuse at passers by, who were all taking hasty avoiding action. Then he caught sight of me and started weaving his way towards the car, shaking his fist in a very menacing manner.

It all happened so quickly, that I didn't have time to wind up the window, and was feeling more than a little scared, when a large head came down over my shoulder, and just as the fellow reached the window he was confronted by two staring eyes and a warning growl. He stopped short, then backed away, but not until he was well clear did Bron lift his head. When my husband returned, you can be sure that Bron was fussed over and given extra treats. After this, I would go anywhere with Bron beside me."

From our RSPCA friends we regularly hear heart warming stories of animals rescued from the most unpleasant circumstances imaginable and there is a group of people whom one might think would be the last of those who might be influenced to take on the responsibility of establishing the pet-person relationship simply because they know too much. At most animal Rescue, Humane, or Care centres you will find a dedicated band of volunteers who 'help out' by freely giving many hours of assistance to the professional staff. Assistance as simple perhaps as taking dogs for a walk. Those who have devoted themselves to the voluntary work for many years can tell some stories that make you feel ashamed to be a human, and others that inspire hope for the future, if we learn from our animal companions. For all their experience and knowledge, however, these volunteers can never be certain that they will not be among the chosen ones themselves, one day, even if they might consider themselves above the influence of emotions that might affect many of us. S & C B were ones who succumbed;

"From the moment he looked at us with his big brown doleful eyes we were lost. We were walking him with other greyhounds at the Little Valley Centre, in Devon, England. Neither of us are really doggie people but we had once looked after a greyhound and had liked the breed for their gentleness and quietness.

Jed has more than fulfilled our faith in greyhounds. We walked him for about six weeks while the staff checked him for catability and for houseability. He was given the go-ahead for

adoption, with the caveat - keep an eye on him! As soon as he entered our house he took over our lives. He has never misbehaved in the house and if anything the three cats chase him. In fact they play and live happily together either walking in the fields or sitting in front of the fire.

Knowledge of the breed is needed. Greyhounds appear self-centred and unemotional, but really need lots of love. Even a short parting is ended with an enormous wagging of the tail. They tend not to be greedy eaters - an advantage. Jed has shown scars from his past. He hates anger and anything raised above his head however innocent makes him cringe. One wonders what had happened to him in his previous two years. But now he is putting on weight, is growing back the hair on his tummy and loves running in the fields."

Lightning, it is said, never strikes twice in the same place but then, fortunately, TLC isn't at all like lightning; or is it? A flash of lightning is over in an instant but can leave marks that last for years. Decisions about TLC can be made in an instant, but bring joy that lasts for years; and they are decisions that can strike twice. P G did not have far to go from her Devon home to find a friend in need, indeed, she had hardly to step out of he door.

"The first dog to choose our home was Robbie, who sadly is no longer with us.

He lived in our road and whilst he did not appear to be badly treated, he was shut out by his owner every day to roam the street and he slept on sacking in a shed. This was many years ago, and at that time the refuse collectors were on strike. Consequently, bin bags and dustbins were left in the road. Robbie had a daily round of bins to find food.

At that time we had a Border Collie and Robbie used to wait until we had been for our walk and would then follow us back to our house although he would never come in. One morning he appeared on our doorstep to show us a cut paw. The same evening I happened to read the pets column in the Express and Echo - "Home wanted for 9 months old collie cross ". We immediately decided that as Robbie had chosen us, we would not let him down. He became a memorable part of our lives until his sad death at the age of 13 years.

The second dog to choose us, Tara, a Labrador, appeared in our lives one very wet March morning. She had been abandoned in the garden of an empty house in our road. She was about 4 months old and had obviously been a Christmas present, now unwanted and thrown out. I had taken our Border Collie and Robbie out for their morning walk when I spotted her. She was very frightened, cold, wet and hungry. I took my dogs home, intending to go back for her, but, unknown to me, she followed me home and hid in the bushes in the front garden.

On going out again, she ran into the road and led me back to the empty house. I brought her home, informed the police and made the usual enquiries, but no one claimed her. Although we had two dogs, both were middle-aged, and we decided to keep her - a decision we never regretted. She is now 8 years old and has given us so much love and gratitude."

The Eyes Have It

Look into their eyes and you will see
That animals have feelings like you and me
They know what is love,
They know what is fear
And one or the other, very clear
Will show in their eyes
When a human draws near.

Look into their eyes and when you see
Their fear of humans like you and me
Treat them with kindness
And love, to remove fear
So that both of those, very clear
They will see in your eyes
As their friend draws near

Look into their eyes and then you'll see
A welcome for humans like you and me
The reflection of trust
An absence of fear;
Loyalty and love, so very clear
Will show in all eyes
When companions draw near.

RR.

Chapter 3

Encounters Across the Rainbow Bridge

The experiences of many people seriously questions the premise that human companionship with pets is restricted to 'until death do us part.' Often, those who share their experiences with us preface their comments with remarks which clearly indicate that they are not confirmed believers in an after-life and/or that they certainly haven't followed a path that may be associated with 'Spiritual Awareness' or 'Enlightenment' in any shape or form.

Many who contact us give no indication of their own beliefs, others express strong opinions, some of which are exact opposites. Few will doubt that a strength of love continues between the person and a departed pet no matter what the beliefs of the person are. For us, how that strength of love is understood, and what form its takes are subjects worth exploring, to the full. We have no objection to minds that close along the way, other than to ask, "if you never open a book, how are you going to learn to read?"

For those who are prepared to consider the suggestion, "books that exist might be worth opening," might also consider the question, "if companionship does not continue in a Spirit World, why do some non-believers wonder if pets and people return across the Rainbow Bridge at times, together?"

Those who believe, already know, and are unlikely to be dissuaded in any way; those who question, are those we happily journey with. As a first step, why is it that many people consider that their present pet receives the approval or even the guidance of a dearly loved one that has journeyed on? M A F, who lives in Scotland first provides us with something to consider;

"Pusskins my black cat was suddenly taken ill and after nursing him for two weeks the vet said that nothing more could be done for him so to save him further suffering we had him put to sleep. Sadly this was rather a messy event since his veins had collapsed and it had to be done into his kidneys as I gently held him. We brought him home and since I could not stand the thought of him being alone I put him in the bedroom where he used to sleep with us every night prior to burying him in the garden. It had been a very upsetting year with my father dying as a result of a bad car crash which left my mother invalided and I was lying in bed beside my sleeping husband at about four o'clock in the morning having a little bubble to myself when suddenly I felt the familiar weight on my bed of Pusskins and the room was filled with the most triumphant and happy purrs totally unlike the strained and forced purr of the previous two weeks.

This lasted for about five minutes before it gently faded away. It was if he had come back to tell me that all was well with him. I will never forget the difference it made to me. Pusskins was special since he chose us and not we him. We

live in the country and watched him "casing the joint" before he decided it was suitable. Shortly before he arrived on the scene we had lost our other cat. Perhaps he had been told of the "vacancy"."

M A F's letter may well have been included by us in an area of our research concerned with the way our pets choose us, had it not been for her last four words, 'told of the 'vacancy'. Even when sharing her loss of Pusskins with us, and her own situation too, it is her bridge of memory that takes us all back to the scene when Pusskins first 'cased' the joint before taking up residence. Is that memory then illuminated by another light, and do her words, 'told of the vacancy' take on a rainbow hue, perhaps?

If Pusskins was told of the vacancy, then was it the previous resident that did the telling? Shortly before Pusskins had arrived at MAF's home she had lost her other cat. Did Pusskins then, learn of the vacancy, from across the rainbow bridge? Reject totally, accept fully, remain undecided, whatever we think about an after-life, and the potential for a rainbow bridge, the loss of a companion can often leave us feeling that we would be breaking the bond between us if we tried to replace a loved one. Is it our loyalty that makes us determined not to let them go or seek another?

Near one of England's ancient university cities the memory bond felt by D J B a few years ago when she lost her friend, 'Toby' made her determined to alter her outlook on pets, and life, completely.

"All my married life we have had a cat, four in all., even when our two boys were young, the last cat was black with a tiny white bib and a white spot on his tummy, called Toby. In February he became ill and despite many visits to the vet he slowly got worse and was losing his dignity, which was distressing for him, he was put to sleep in August, he was only

12 years old not a great age for a cat. After his death we all felt and "saw" Toby many times in the house and garden, he left a presence.

My husband and I decided that we would not have another cat as Toby's death was a very sad and moving experience, we felt that we would never get over or replace the love and affection he gave us. We decided that we would adopt a dog as we had the energy and lifestyle to give a dog a suitable home. Off we went to the local Blue Cross filled in the necessary paperwork gave our details etc. we were told we have the "perfect cat" for you. Yes we did look at dogs, but we could feel "Ozzie" pulling us his way, when we met him it was love at first sight, we were lucky and were allowed to bring him home the same day.

As soon as Ozzie entered the house we felt a peace as if Toby approved and his Ghost was laid to rest. Ozzie is a cross between a Bengal and an Abyssinian, and, yes he has settled in beautifully."

D J B's energy and lifestyle may well have been more than adequate to ensure that a dog companion would have welcomed an opportunity to live with such a sharing couple. Yet, when a companion comes your way, or is guided towards you, there seems little to be done other than to enjoy the guidance given. And sometimes that can seem endless enjoyment, as it was for C E B of Essex.

"One day I was laying on the sofa, half dozing, when Florence, my cat, jumped up on the arm behind my head. She put her nose down my ear and purred loudly, wanting petting. I duly responded and stroked her head and rubbed her ears.

We lay like that for a minute or two, me stroking her, her purring, and flexing her feet, when I remembered that Florence had been 'dead' for 3 months now. I lay there, still stroking, but now thinking furiously, could it be my neighbour's cat? No,

I recognised Florence's purr. Well, what should I do? I finally decided I had to look, but as I turned nothing was there and all feeling and purring stopped. It may have been an hallucination of course. I know how real they can seem, but I choose to think not. It was too real for too long. As far as I'm concerned Florence came to say goodbye."

The most natural of responses from C E B in an everyday situation only altered when she realized that Florence and she had been separated for a few months, but she still had no doubt about the reason for Florence's visit.

Mrs E H B from Hertfordshire had been used to having pets for most of her life and when lost 'Bo' after cancer was found in his front leg she remembered her lovely $15\frac{1}{2}$ years old Welsh Boarder collie as having been quite exceptional. He was also remembered for his beauty, for being loving and good, and as a companion who gave her no worry. She also had no doubt about the future, and got another dog from the rescue centre.

"Although he does not replace Bo he is a dear. Now the first dream I had of Bo was he was laying in the garden by our back door, it was pouring with rain.

I opened the door and I said "I'm sorry pet you will soon be going." I phoned my niece in this dream and asked her if she could do anything for him. She said she will pick him up. I said if he comes back do not let him walk and she said I will bring him back in the car.

It was so real and he was just the same as he was - black and white and beautiful. The second dream was so strange. He was in half, no inclination of a dog. He was just grey but I knew it was him. Chum, our present dog was in the distance. I hope there is a meaning to this."

After 15¹/₂ years together, could it be that the Rainbow Bridge was a bridge too far for Bo to race over without letting his dearest friend know where he was going? And was the presence of Chum, the successor of Bo, just a glimpse for Mrs E H B of one friend bidding farewell to another?

It has become a privilege for us to hear from those who want to share their experiences and do so even when even simple tasks become a problem. In her Midlands home, writing became a problem for D W H after she suffered a stroke, but this did not deter her from sharing these words with us.

"May I tell you about the 3 returns of my beloved Akba? He died 3 years ago at the age of 8 from FeLV. I was totally devastated - I've always had a multi-cat family, but Akky was my No 1 son (and I still miss him, even though I now know he's always with me).

Seven weeks after his death, I had a stroke. Whilst lying in bed one day I felt fur under my affected hand, stroked it and was rewarded by purring. Opening my eyes to see who it was I found the bed empty, none of my others was there. 2¹/₂ years on, I took in a big gaunt black stray.

One day I opened the door for him to go out, and looked at the narrow shelf on which he was resting, saying "Come on Pharaoh" - but it was Akky sitting there. I did a double take, said "Akky - you're back". Then suddenly it was Pharaoh again. There was no similarity between them apart from size - Akky was a brown/grey tabby with yellow eyes, Pharaoh was is a British Shorthair, coal black with orange eyes. I'm convinced that Akky was telling me he'd guided Pharaoh to me, and was endorsing his application to stay.

Finally, when Akky's old friend, my beloved Smo became too tired and old to carry on, at age 21, I made an appointment with the vet to put him to sleep. Before we left for that traumatic last journey I took Smo to the back door to have a last look at his garden and there was Akky sitting, waiting to escort his old friend to his new home. It was not another cat - one moment he was there, then he was not.

I believe in life after death, and that I will see all my darlings again. In fact when I had the strokes I was lying on the floor thinking "is this it then?? Great - now I can be with Akky (and Vortigern and Sammy , and Cleo, and Hecate, and Shah..... !) again". It was rather upsetting to find out that I was going to survive after all ! Still, there are the current family to care for, and Akky rewarded me by sending the fabulous Pharaoh. Apologies for the writing, it all went awful after the stroke."

No apologies were needed, of course. Having family knowledge of the limitations a stroke can produce, we appreciate the added need to communicate that D W H that prompted her to tell us of Akky's three happy returns.

In correspondence from a lady who lives in Wales we found the need to communicate taking to extremes, and that the rainbow bridge possessed extraordinary dimension, if dimensions can even be considered, when H K wrote to tell of her experiences after the death of her Persian cat, Shireen.

"I was incredibly close to Shireen, and I used to worry about her constantly as she had poor health following an accident in 1992. In November last year I went to Malta for a week, leaving Shireen at the vet; she had been ill but was quite definitely on the mend. Now, normally once I'm away I don't worry about my cats, but this time was different. It was three days later, I was on Gozo, and I began to get a kind of recurring waking dream about Shireen dying. Over and over again I would see myself arriving back at the airport, contacting the vet, being told she was dead. Eventually the following morning I phoned the vet, hoping to reassure myself, only to be told that Shireen was dying.

I was devastated; here I was thousands of miles from home, with no way to see my cat. I asked to speak to Shireen on the phone, and told her I loved her and said goodbye. The vet told me she had recognised my voice even in her semi-conscious state, and that she seemed very peaceful. After that I went for a walk along the cliffs, feeling empty and very helpless, for there was nothing else I could do.

About half an hour later I felt what I can only describe as a bolt of spiritual energy go through my whole body. It was so intense I had to sit down on the rocks for I could barely move. Everything was extraordinarily bright, and it was as if the whole universe was rejoicing. It seemed connected to Shireen, but at the time I didn't understand why. For some reason I looked at my watch; it was exactly 2 o'clock. Eventually things calmed down and I carried on walking.

Suddenly, about half an hour later, I felt a cat weaving around my bare legs. I looked down, and Shireen jumped up into my arms and began purring loudly. I knew it was her though I could not see her; but I could feel her, and I stroked her as she purred loudly and joyfully. And I noticed she had her tail back, although she'd lost her tail after the accident four years previously. Interestingly, I had no notion that Shireen was dead. Neither did it seem strange to me that she was visiting me on the cliffs in Gozo, thousands of miles from North Wales.
I was simply delighted to see her, and accepted the experience for what it was.

It wasn't until after I got back to the hotel and phoned the vet that I realised what had happened. It turned out that Shireen had died at the exact moment, as far as we could estimate, that I had felt the energy and joy of the universe. It then, somehow, took her half an hour to find me in Gozo. How had she found me, and why?

I felt certain that she had come to say goodbye to me, before going wherever it was she had to go. I also felt sure I would not see her again, for there would be no reason to; for hadn't the universe been rejoicing that she was to go on? This knowledge made her death easier to bear, although being human I missed her horribly, and I still do now. One other thing - at around the same time I also "saw" a little tortie cat bringing me a kitten, which I knew was Shireen in her next life. I spent several months waiting for this to happen, but it hasn't, as yet. But such messages have no time limit, so who knows? Maybe, if it's right.....”

In an interview published in *Your Cat* magazine in December 1997, Evelyn mentioned that there is; "the Buddhist theory that animals are reincarnated through the levels until they eventually return as human beings."

This prompted H K to add;

"One final comment on what you might say about Buddhism (or the quote in Your Cat anyway). In fact, the death of any being may result in the birth of any other being, depending on what is needed. In other words, a cat may be reborn as another cat, or a human being, or almost anything else which is the best way to work out its karma; it is not a case of going up or down through levels. I spent ten years in a Buddhist monastery, and this is my understanding of it anyway. So I'm sure Shireen is where she needs to be, wherever it is. I'm just grateful she came to say goodbye to me first."

A lady, M N, who lives not far from London informed us that she records, on daily basis, any dreams, out of body experiences, and Higher Self communications and that on November 11th, 1993, to end his suffering, she had to have her lovely little dog Jamie put to sleep.

"Jamie was a cross between a corgi (shape) and ears and coat of a black and white spaniel. As always it is traumatic having to make the decision to allow them to move on, and on the day before while writing up my diary I had these beautifully comforting words come through:-

"It is only sad for those left behind, for him it is a release for a shell that doesn't function well any more - love him and send him on his eternal journey and thank him for sharing this time with you. He was here for you. He was sent for you to learn to love. Thank his spirit for his selfless devotion, thank him for all his lessons he has taught you, and love he has given."

I tell you - not a dry eye in the house !!

Then the following evening after he had passed over I received the following:-

"They (the souls of animals) flit back and forth between the lower vibrations for the healing of humanity and the balancing of the Earth. Do not worry he is an eternal being that has been here to help people may times before, he has been here to help people love, that was his job this time."

Four days later I had a "dream" Jamie came back to visit me - I was in bed and he came bounding in to see me, bounced all around on top of the bed so much I had to tell him to calm down. He seemed so happy and full of life - his fur was soft and silky and he looked on 3 - 4 years old. He was wagging his tail and bounced on to my pillow and I told him to get off my pillow, he did and jumped down off the bed to see my three children, Emma, Douglas and Duncan. Then he popped his head above the end of the bed again so full of life and vitality and happiness. Then he was gone.

It left me feeling very happy and I haven't been sad about his loss ever since. He has been back to see me several times since. For quite a while I felt his presence around the house - in the usual homely places. Often there to greet me by the door when I came home just as he used to.

About one month later - roughly - I had another lovely night visit from him. This time he brought a couple of friends along with him to introduce them to me which was lovely, one was a young very ginger brown boxer and the other a white shortish dog of mixed parentage - the boxer particularly was interested in meeting me - another happy occasion.

The other particularly memorable "dream" was when he came back to "see" me (this was only about 8 months ago) to take me on a lovely country walk with him beside a stream and along a track. I remember so clearly the young fresh bright green growth of the young trees and Jamie's lovely silky grey white and black coat. His tail didn't stop wagging the whole time as he ran backwards and forwards and back to me. Wonderful.

A psychic friend of my parents told me that after my father died in '86 they would see him standing at the gate of his old house with two dogs from the farm that had passed over a while before. In his life he had often fed the farm dogs by the gate, they weren't well fed and he had such a love for them. My parents' old dog, a black Labrador that passed on some years before, was around the house for a long time. I remember very clearly crossing the bungalow hallway and caught sight of him in the right corner of my eye ambling down to see me. Of course as soon as I turned my whole head round to see him, I couldn't.

I feel there is no doubt that, just like humans, if you grieve too heavily for the loss of a beloved pet it prevents them moving away and getting on with their next job."

In a letter from a lady living on the eastern side of England we also learned that the loss of a beloved pet can, indeed, have remarkable repercussions for the person who is heart-broken at the loss. While to grieve too heavily may prevent a pet from moving on, the experience of R P-W at the loss of her beloved Rudi, a beautiful sandy and cream cat, was that her intense grief at his parting was enough to put her into hospital.

"Before I left home I 'spoke' to Rudi and asked him to come and see me in hospital. Whilst waiting in the lounge of the hospital for my husband to visit me two days later, I closed my eyes as I didn't want other patients to think that I was listening to their conversations. I must emphasize that I was not asleep as I was well aware of all the chatter. Something

made me open my eyes and as I looked over the arm of the chair, there was Rudi walking past. I spoke to him, and then he was gone.

The second experience was somewhat different. Some months later I was sitting in a chair at my home, thinking of nothing in particular and listening to my neighbour hammering as he erected a new fence. Suddenly I was no longer in my chair but in the extension we had built for Rudi and I was looking through the wire talking to my neighbour's cat, Emma. I couldn't believe my eyes when Rudi appeared and stood beside Emma.

I said "Oh, Rudi."

He looked all golden with the sun on him. His colouring had always been beautiful but in those few seconds he was really glowing. He stood there looking at me. Then with a slight jolt (I can't describe it in any other way) I was back in my chair. I was quite taken aback at what had happened as I'd always been a little wary (or sceptical) when I'd heard these things happening.

A medium explained that what happened on the second occasion I saw Rudi was an out-of-body experience. Again I must add that I was not asleep, as through the whole experience I heard my neighbour using his hammer. It was even louder when I was talking to Emma and Rudi because I was closer to the noise."

From among the letters, facsimiles, and e-mails that fill our files we recognize that individuals who find that they have to try come to terms with something they may not understand, nor want to even consider believing, still remain adamant about what they have experienced, and what they alone can know is a truth. When something happens to a family, the experience is shared but is the truth more easily accepted?

J R R once lived in a London borough and wrote to put on record that it is undeniable that something unexplained happened to her and her family during the time they lived in a small terraced house in Battersea.

"Shortly after moving in in 1976 I had the job of removing building rubble and trench digging the small back yard in order to remove years of underground weed roots and rubbish and to turn it into an attractive little garden. While doing this I unearthed something which looked like an animal skeleton and my husband said it was the remains of a cat. I believe I reburied these at the time, though I can't be sure now, and I was sad to have disturbed the remains of someone's once loved pet. However it passed out of my mind, but later I remembered it as I had cause to wonder if the incident perhaps triggered the experiences we as a family had later, and for the rest of the eight years we lived there.

I recall that, walking through the tiny narrow hallway one evening just by the side of the staircase and next to the radiator, I almost tripped over a small dark coloured animal which I saw so clearly that my reflexes made me stop and tread over it as one would do to step over a family pet in a confined space, but at a second glance there was nothing there. Thinking my mind had been playing me tricks I forgot it, but a week or so later it happened again and then my husband

rather cautiously mentioned to me that he had thought he'd seen a cat in the hall a few times out of the corner of his eye, but no cat was really there. I had not said anything to him at all, but then did so and really did begin to wonder what was happening.

In any event we never spoke about it to anyone else and from time to time both caught glances of our seemingly unearthly little visitor. We had a dog at the time and she never seemed to show any obvious signs of seeing a cat in her house.

We eventually got a real cat of our own when our daughter Lucy was two, and when nearing her third birthday. She came to me one day and said that she had tried to stroke 'Emma' in the hall, and it wasn't Emma, and it disappeared !

Lucy was very bright for her age and not prone to imagining things and we of course had not mentioned our experiences to her. She mentioned other experiences over the next few years and said that the strange cat rubbed against her legs sometimes. Finally, and to my mind furthering the evidence of a supernatural experience, for what else could it be? During the summer one year my niece, then fourteen, came to stay for a few days, and one evening she visibly jumped and looked very perplexed. I asked her what was wrong - she said that as she was sitting with Lucy on the settee she looked straight at a black cat on the arm of the settee and it had disappeared before her eyes.

We then told her about it and all discussed what we had experienced - had it been the result of disturbing the pet's grave, was something already there before that perhaps - in fact, what was it all about? I can never really explain why or how, but until we left the house, the 'cat' occasionally was seen around and I wonder if it is still there. This is a true account and not in the least embellished.

In that terraced home in Battersea, in a very short period of time, different generations shared experiences that many people will not encounter in a lifetime. Whatever the reality of the Rainbow Bridge, it is there for all ages to find, and apparently can be experienced by all age groups. Whether or not to recognize the Rainbow Bridge, or try to determine what it is, may well be things that we each have to decide for ourselves.

The question is, are those with experience any more able to recognize the Rainbow Bridge than those of us who seek to learn?

A C P lives on the South coast and many years ago was given the gift of a puppy. 'Sadie' was a cross between a Labrador and a mongrel, and became a lovely lady who proved to a valued companion and a darling dog that was very well behaved throughout the time she and A C P lived together.

"When she reached 12 years old, she was ready to return to Spirit. I have worked for Spirit as a medium and healer for over 40 years, so I have had many wonderful experiences, and so there is much I have learnt about animals. They all have a counterpart, just as all life on earth has a counterpart. I was told by my teachers that if I took care of Sadie and she

progressed sufficiently, in her next life she would be ready for human form.

When Sadie passed, Spirit informed me that she would be used in America with the police dogs helping to sniff out the drugs etc. A handler would bring her to me from time to time which made us both so happy.

After 6 years she was brought to

England to work and after being in Spirit for 10 years she was then being prepared for the human form, 2 years ago she was born into China as a female. Perhaps when I return to Spirit I shall be able to see her, my family all loved her so much.

This house here that I live in is a power house. I know so many public figures who are brought here to regenerate before moving on to their rightful place, there are always Spirit animals running up and down my stairs. A crocodile is often brought here to find out the overloaded spots of power in this room. I have also seen a huge Spirit tarantula walking up the side of my son's face to find the communicating lines which are as fine as a spider's web. So much that I can tell you I have been hugged by monkeys and stroked their silken coat, touched a huge snake to overcome my fear.

All sorts of animals have been in this house brought by the teachers as a protection on their journey. If only everyone would know of this truth there would be less cruelty towards all animals and they would be loved and helped on their way to progression."

Another lady from London, M D L, has written of her experiences, some of which we shall include elsewhere but, in 1975 she had several cats, one of which was a Siamese sealpoint named Bongo whom, apparently, had many friends.

"Bongo was a wonderful cat but he had an irritating habit of crawling up beside your head and licking your ears until he drove us crazy. We couldn't have him in bed with us because he'd lick ears all night if we'd let him so Bongo spent every night exiled to the living room. All the same we loved him and were greatly grieved when I found him one day lying dead under an Oleander bush. Obviously he had chewed on the leaves and poisoned himself.

About a month later our other Siamese gave birth to five kittens. One of them was a beautiful male sealpoint. When he was three weeks old and could barely walk, I had him and the other kittens in the living room with me but I wasn't really paying attention to them as I was watching TV, lying on the floor.

Suddenly I felt something warm and wet moving in and out of my ear in a hauntingly familiar way. I put my hand to my ear in shock. It was the little sealpoint who had crept over on his shaky little legs to lick my ears. I knew (with a rather eerie feeling) that this was Bongo come back to me and this was his way of letting me know. I have read that if dogs or cats make especial spiritual progress with one person or family, they return again and again to the family."

To that we can only add, that it is with the help of M D L, and others who communicate with us that we'll find out; and even then we have to try to decide from which side of the Rainbow Bridge the guidance is coming from.

RUDI

He came to us a little stray
And made it clear he was here to stay.
His bright blue eyes in his little face
Told us everywhere was his special place.

He was not the cat who walked alone,
He loved the place which was his home
Our Rudi with his endearing ways
Gave us so many happy days.

As he grew his eyes changed from blue to gold,
With his love of life, he never grew old.
Ever the playful kitten, playing with sunbeams on the floor,

Yet still very much the boss of the house,
As he came stalking through the door.

He loved a special toy and he loved to make it squeak,
When he succeeded, what would he have said, if he could only speak !
He often made us laugh as he scampered up the hall,
Rather like an excited dog chasing after his ball.

He was very proud of his coat, which he loved to clean,
It was silky, so beautiful, all sandy and cream.
He shared his love with us equally,
Sleeping sometimes with Peter, and sometimes with me.

Now after so many happy years,
We are alone with memories, and often tears.
Yet we know we are not really all alone,
Rudi often visits us and his home.

Then he goes back to his heavenly home, not very far away,
And he waits for us and that happy day,
When we go to join him, never again to part,
With our beloved Rudi so close to our heart.

R P-W

Chapter 4

How Close Can We Get To The Kindred Spirit of A Pet?

When humans have brought about their own demise, and we surely will, Mother Nature will gather her small Angels together, and the Circle of Life will begin all over again.

Already, in preparation perhaps, many humans identify more readily, and certainly more appreciatively, with animals other than those of their own kind. It is sometimes said that an animals' human companion, or owner as they are sometimes called, can become so close to their pets that a physical resemblance can be seen.

For any reader who could readily identify such 'twinning' among their friends or acquaintances, we would suggest that it is quite probable that the owners of those pets may not quite agree with the premise entirely but would, perhaps, recognize that the affinity they share with a beloved pet goes far beyond the casual acquaintanceship created by simple ownership. Such an affinity, relationship,. bond, call it what you will, has at its base one simple thing; trust. On a foundation of trust all things can grow; friendship, consideration, companionship, reliability, loyalty, love.

On a warm, sunny, morning in 1993, J P of Woodbridge, hardly expected a close encounter she experienced with a pair of kittens to affect her family, or that it could provide an insight for others into the process of animal/human bonding that clearly reveals the need for trust; and the methods employed to establish it.

On the odd occasion during the previous two weeks or so, JP had seen a black stray timidly darting about her garden and thought nothing of it, until equally timid offspring ventured on to the patio. As she busied herself in her kitchen, through the window she caught a glimpse of two tiny adventurers, a pair of beautiful kittens; one coal black, one with white feet, nose and bib.

They were sitting there like a pair of almost perfectly matched book ends. It was as if they had suddenly materialized from nowhere, and she hardly dared move. But they knew she was there, watching; and the trust began. Their green eyes, wide open and unblinking, stared back at her as she thrilled to their presence, and appreciated their beauty, fearing tho' that if she moved towards them, or even blinked, they would just as suddenly disappear.

JP was accustomed to having animals, and all kind of creatures, visit the garden she enjoyed with her husband and family and was first to admit that;

"Even our best friends would be hard put to call our garden well trimmed. If our village entered the Britain In Bloom contest, a working party would have to be formed to put it in order so that we would not let the side down.

We prefer to think of it as an eco-friendly wild garden; our pond harbours frogs, and as of this year, a newt; we see lots of butterflies and bees among the mass of rosemary, lavender, marjoram, sage and mint; hedgehogs overwinter in the piles of wood and leaves, and - until 1993 - it was open house for birds. We watched fascinated as a pair of spotted flycatchers raised their brood of three successfully in a terracotta wall pot on the side of the house, and were privileged to see the first flight of the fledglings; each year we have witnessed the frantic activity of nesting bluetits.

But, of course, the very attractions which bring the insects and small animals, also brought, we believe, a pregnant Mumsie, who probably used our large woodpile as a nursery, and a convenient place to find the odd meal of shrews and mice. My husband, Robin, has never been very keen on cats, but even he was interested in these little creatures who had magically appeared."

The relationship JP intended to have, or imagined she was to have, with the kittens was one she considered would be short lived. As the two furry bundles gazed up at her she innocently believed that she could best help by catching them and passing them on to the RSPCA or the Cat's Protection League for neutering and homing. Well aware of her husband's antipathy to cats, she had thought of keeping the kittens but, when she resolved to put food out for them, considered her act of kindness only as a means of gaining their confidence in order to help them even more.

What her kind heart had not taken into account was the personality possessed by each of the kittens she intended to set safely upon the road to eventual 'rescue,' or the affect the developing personalities of the kittens would have on other members of her family who began to take an interest in their well-being.

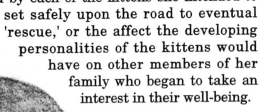

"At first, I put bowls of food, morning and evening where I had seen them, gradually moving them closer to the

house, and finally into the porch. The kittens would appear, as if by magic, and it wasn't for several days that I realized that they were silently watching me from under the low, arching branches of a cotoneaster, growing at the edge of the patio.

All I could see was two pairs of green eyes, moving in unison, their black coats indiscernible against the shadowy background. Their mother kept well away; it was almost as if she brought them to us, watched to see we had taken responsibility, and left. Then, one day, after several weeks, I saw three pairs of watchful eyes under the bush; she had returned.

By this time, Socks was showing herself to be the most trusting. She would let me stroke her, and she made one or two forays indoors. Sooty allowed me near - but would not be touched."

The foundation of trust can be clearly seen in this developing relationship and, upon it already, the seeds of friendship were being sown; which intrigued and attracted the mother of the kittens, and began to have an affect upon JP's own children.

"Mumsie - as she was by then called - came to eat with her kittens, never on her own, and disappeared quickly. As they seemed pretty independent, and knowing if he wanted a quiet life he would have to give in to the children's pleas, Robin came round to the idea of letting them stay. Before he could change his mind, a cat flap was fitted in our porch, which all three mastered in minutes."

On to that foundation of trust the family had established with Mumsie and her kittens they now added 'companionship,' through their ever open door, or at least an easily opened cat-flap, and 'consideration' for their new companions came quite naturally in the progression of things.

"The next problem was neutering. By this time it was December, and I felt that Mumsie should be spayed as soon as possible. I borrowed a trap from the CPL., and still not able to approach her closely, spent ages outside one wet and blowy night setting it with tempting food. It was so sensitive that it trapped my arm twice, and once, when set, the wind caused it to fall. Mumsie, however, walked into it, ate the food and backed out delicately without, it seemed, the slightest risk of trapping herself.

Successful on the second night, she was operated on and back within a day. Sooty and Socks, spayed in February, were much easier to catch. It was a simple task to lure the trusting Socks, and where she went, Sooty followed, especially if food was involved.

Since then, they have grown much more trusting and confident, enjoying our company and giving us quite a few laughs. Socks loves to sleep on top of the video player.

Sooty can't resist a newspaper on the floor - she crawls under it and seems to enjoy the rustling noise and the feel of it.

Mumsie has always been the most timid, and for a long time she would not venture into the house. I often wonder what brought her to us in the first place. Did she run away, get lost, or was she abandoned? Whatever her origin and background, she was extremely timid, deeply mistrustful, and always alert in the presence of people, usually making a run for it if any of us went too close. She maintained this distance from us until May 1995."

It was on the Bank Holiday Monday that Mumsie failed to appear for breakfast or supper and, concerned by her absence, an increasingly worried JP went out into the garden and around the area searching for her and calling her by name; but to no avail. Of the timid cat she had taken into her home, there was no sign. Was it that Mumsie had decided to move on, she wondered? Then other thoughts also entered her head. Could Mumsie have been involved in an accident? Was she lying out there somewhere, beside the road perhaps, in need of help? JP was starting to prepare herself for the worst when, in the mid-evening, Mumsie re-appeared.

"She came in through the cat flap, staggering, with a woefully shattered tail. She was pitifully pleased to see us, purring and lying down immediately on the blanket we put out for her. How she managed to return home at all we shall never cease to find amazing in view of her life threatening injuries."

Mumsie's injuries were certainly life threatening, so, is it possible, or probable that loyalty was the spiritual influence that guided Mumsie home that night? Loyalty that was two-fold?

Despite her injuries Mumsie loyally returned to her own kittens. Because of her injuries she returned to the human companions who had shown her friendship and consideration, shared companionship with her, proved their reliability and, when it was most needed, would demonstrate their loyalty.

Mumsie was rushed to the Vet who confirmed that her injuries were consistent with being run over. Apart from her injured tail, spinal damage was feared and she had sustained internal injuries that had split her diaphragm and were causing breathing difficulties for her.

Confident that he could help Mumsie overcome these problems, the vet was less certain that she would regain bowel or bladder control. Another test of loyalty for JP and her family perhaps who could do nothing more but to await developments. Mumsie remained at the vet's and every day JP telephoned for news. The answer was always the same - no result yet. It was a week before Mumsie recovered sufficiently for the vet to consider she could go home; to the home filled with great rejoicing when she came back to convalesce in a hastily erected pen in the garage. Everyone was amazed at the dignity and fortitude Mumsie showed throughout her ordeal.

"She never complained, scratched or bit, and was so pleased to be home at last that she purred continuously and even climbed on to my lap. I felt really honoured that she had learned to trust us enough to ask for our help at her time of need. She quickly regained her strength, and when it was clear that she was going to make a full recovery, she was operated on again to remove her damaged tail.

In the following months, she has become much more domesticated, spending part of every day and most of the evening indoors.

She is not a "hearthrug" cat, usually selecting a far corner of the room under a chair, but during the day, when the house is quiet, she can often be found curled up comfortably on the sofa."

Mumsie had undoubtedly found 'love' and there can also be no doubt that JP's close encounter with a pair of kittens on that warm, sunny morning in 1993 confirms that on a foundation of trust all things can grow; friendship, consideration, companionship, reliability, loyalty and, not least of all, love. It must more than probable that every member of JP's family gained from the encounter, and continue to do so; as do Mumsie and her, now grown, kittens about which JP must have the last word.

"At night all three sleep heaped up together, indiscernible one from another, in an old dog basket in the porch, a glistening, rippling, satin-black three headed, twelve legged monster, with just 20 lives and two tails left!"

For some of us the passing of time clouds the memory, for others it clears the mind. JP, her husband, and their children are not likely to forget any incident that involved them, individually or collectively, with their beloved cats.

Even though many years have passed by since the events CL from County Durham related to us occurred, they are still very clear in her mind too. Many years ago, in 1970 to be precise, she took in a young pregnant, black and white, feral cat that her mother decided to call Cleopatra, usually abbreviated to Cleo, because of the sphinx-like mystic manner the cat maintained.

Cleo lived with CL and her mother for $8^{1}/_{2}$ years, but towards the end of that time Cleo suffered a lengthy period of debilitating illness. She was diagnosed as suffering from cancer which, to the consternation of her human companions, travelled up her spine and paralysed her back legs.

Together, mother and daughter made the ultimate decision for their friend. In the final act of kindness they could show her, they agreed that Cleo must be relieved of her suffering and put to sleep but, with Cleo's passing, CL's story does not end. As the years passed by, her thoughts would sometimes return to the cat she had loved dearly and in 1981, in what she calls, 'a vision,' she held Cleo in her arms again.

"I was stroking her and running my fingers through her coat. I can still remember being impressed by the softness of her fur. I thought nothing of this at the time but in retrospect I believe it was an omen:- Later that year I was asked by a work colleague if I would like a kitten.

I declined his offer but a few days later another colleague, during a phone call with him, jokingly said that I'd changed my mind and handed me the phone. Unintentionally and quite impulsively I accepted and requested "a refined lady companion" to which he informed me that my choice was limited to the runt of the litter, a tiny black and white one as the remainder were all males.

I arranged to collect 'her' the following day from his home. He tried very hard and with various tactics to dissuade me from my choice and I had to admit that 'she' (Suzy) was the smallest and least attractive out of the rainbow of colours available.

However, I stuck to my guns and also chose a companion to keep 'her' company while I was out at work. Timmy was the most handsome of cats; tabby and white but as totally shy, nervous and introverted as Suzy was bold, happy and extroverted."

For the first few weeks CL found herself calling Suzy "Cleo" and had to persist to break the habit. It didn't help when she found out that Suzy was, in fact, a 'he'.

He was a very happy little chap, purring constantly (even with his mouth full) and able to cope with any eventuality, being completely unafraid. He was often observed high overhead, on patrol at roof level, or balanced precariously, yet nonchalantly, at the top of some scaffolding wherever builders were at work.

"Often as I dug the garden he would accompany me digging holes with his paws, (giving me a hand). As he was slight in build it was easy for him to run up my jeans onto my back or shoulders and as I moved around I just folded my arms behind me and carrying him, continued what I was doing. I had a cat flap fitted but it was unused when I was at home apart from being knocked for me to go and let him in. He was so intelligent he seemed to be the 'superman' of the cat world.

Early in 1984 I began to get the impression that something wonderful was going to happen at the time of the full moon in May and as the date approached, the feeling intensified and I became more and more excited, hardly able to contain myself at this then unknown prospect.

As I prepared to go bed that night, the 14th of May 1984, the night of a full moon, I looked for Suzy on the window-sill behind the curtains, his usual place. He wasn't there but the door to the porch was ajar and I found him already waiting at the front door to let him out.

When her cat named Suzy didn't return next morning CL became concerned because his absence was unusual; he never stayed away. As the hours passed by, both she and Timmy became increasingly anxious, each watching, waiting, and listening; but of their mutual friend Suzy, there was no sign.

"As I watched the tea-time news on TV, a clock on top of the set shot forward and fell on the floor. Later a bottle of shampoo fell into the bath; later still a coat hanger fell from a hook behind the bathroom door. On both occasions the noise attracted my attention and attendance, as I wasn't present when either item fell. I can clearly remember thinking to myself, "that's funny, three things have fallen and I wasn't near any of them."

69

That night in bed a vision unfolded of a landscape made up of glistening silver light. Everything, the whole environment, was made of this silver light: sky, grass, flowers, shrubs, trees, rushes in a large pond on the surface of which Suzy was slowly walking, having a sniff here and a few laps of water there. Effortlessly walking on the trunks of large trees and among the branches. His mood was very quiet and subdued as he explored his new surroundings."

If this had been but a dream or even an occasional passing thought of her absent cat, it might have been a dream or thought easily forgotten. Next morning, Suzy was still absent but the memories remained. That night CL witnessed again the same silver landscape, the pond, the trees, and Suzy. His mood remained subdued; he walked with the same, slow, effortless movements. He was alone.

"On the third night I was reading in bed and looked up to see Suzy bounding towards me full of life and energy, just as he always was. I was 'caught up in the scene' and I opened my

arms to catch him when he jumped (he always did take a run and a jump despite my screams of protest) saying "You little devil, I thought you were dead." Simultaneously as I closed my arms around him both Suzy and the vision were gone - abruptly - he never landed in my arms, to my surprise.

It must have taken him 3 days to realize his state and pass through the astral plane to his true spiritual home, then come to tell me, (back from the heart of God). I know nothing happens by chance - 'not a sparrow falls'. Do you think Cleo came back to complete her evolution as a cat?"

To CL it is obvious, in retrospect, that Suzy had attained all he could in that particular life as a cat and as he was unable to progress further on this level of consciousness in which she was his companion he had returned to his spiritual home to await his next incarnation; but not before he had let her know.

To the story of her encounter CL added an unrelated postscript, well, almost unrelated as it doesn't concern a spiritual return or indicate how close we can get to the spirit of a kindred pet; or does it?

"My cat Tigger was lying on the bed beside me one night and I hadn't the heart to disturb her when I settled for sleep, as she was so snug and comfortable. It was quite dark but I could see her outline as she lay there and there seemed to be something around her neck. I reached out and took hold of what appeared to be a cord, working it round until a label appeared (a Paddington Bear label). On this label, in letters of light, was written "Made By God".

The confirmation of an encounter that we received from PG of Manchester, however, serves to illustrate that a beloved pet that is truly a kindred spirit, will show consideration for its human companion, as clearly as any human would show it for the animal with which they have forged an eternal bond. Emma, was a beautiful dog, a curly coated retriever that PG adored, a companion who became very close to her.

"She would sit next to me on the settee with her head on my shoulder. There was a very strong bond. She was five years old when she died suddenly of a brain tumour. She waited until I was away one weekend, and just went."

Before continuing with PG's letter, just let us consider those last few words again; *'She waited until I was away one weekend, and just went.'*

When we read them for the first time, it seemed a matter-of-fact statement that could have described many a human 'parting of the ways.' A leaving home, that was intended to hurt; A love, broken beyond repair, had ended in a hurried, unseen, departure; A carefully planned achievement, to avoid tears and woe; In human terms, selfless consideration came last in our list and yet where none other could be applied to the action taken by the kindred spirit that PG knew and loved as Emma, a retriever, we suggest that it is the recognition by PG that Emma 'waited' for her to be away one week-end that confirms the bond that existed between them, and that both were aware of that bond.

Did Emma, in choosing her day of departure,

show consideration for her human companion and try to minimize the pain she knew her friend would feel?

When PG returned home and found that Emma had died, she was absolutely devastated. She did have another companion, another older dog, but the bond between them was not the strong bond she had shared with Emma, whom she did not intend to try and replace.

The memories of her were strong as she recalled in her letter that the retriever had had a bed in the kitchen, next to the vegetable rack, and told us how Emma would take carrots out of it and put them between her paws and chew them.

A few months after Emma's death PG heard from a friend who told her that her dog had escaped whilst in season and had unexpectedly had pups, and asked if PG would I like to visit her, and see them. PG responded without hesitation;

"I love pups so off I went. I saw one little white ball of fluff with black spotted ears and picked her up and said I will have this one when she is old enough.

When she was six weeks I went to collect her and brought her into the house, put her down in a large strange house. She walked straight into the kitchen, sat on Emma's ex-bed, took a carrot out of the vegetable rack and gave me such a knowing look! I immediately hugged her and said, you have come back! She is Tara and she has been a most beautiful loyal friend. She has always been so good and is like Emma in so many ways.

One other thing, just after Emma died a lady who knew me vaguely and who has psychic ability phoned me and said, "Has your dog died, only I have received a message to say that she will come back to you!"

It is not unusual, we have come to realize, that whatever a person expects from a pet/person relationship it is not always, or even often, that the person decides how that relationship is to be established, or whom it will include. From a friendly contact in the USA we learned that N E M had experienced many encounters through her many pet/person contacts.

"I got Noelani Misty BabyCat when Ariadne was 17 years old. She was the first other cat that Ari ever truly accepted. (You'll meet Ariadne later) Miss BabyCat was born a feral cat, and I adopted her when she was 4 weeks old. She was often sick, for the first $3^{1}/_{2}$ years I had her with one respiratory infection after another, I almost lost her one night when I thought she had stopped breathing. My sister rushed us to pet emergency, some 25 miles away. Thankfully, they stabilized her and sent us home.

The next day I went to a new vet, and after massive doses of antibiotics the whole summer BabyCat got well. I also did white light treatments on her; I would empty my mind and let this incredible light flow through me, through my hands and into her body. Well, she did get well, and in fact will be celebrating her 11th birthday on April 16th. She is my happy little BabyCat.

I have always had this real rapport with animals, and especially cats, and I have always had this healing ability. It is just the neatest feeling, But of course it is not something I normally talk about, Most people would think I am bonkers,

In the summer of 1992, 1 went to the door to call my two little black kittens in. That was Shadesie and Arabella. Well, it was dark and the lights were off, and two little dark kittens bounded in when I called. When I turned on the light I was surprised to find they weren't "my" kittens at all, but two little Tortis. Well I did adopt them. I call them my Star Kittens, because I believe they fell from the stars. My little Altair

Leilani, and Deneb Hokule'a, (Heavenly Flower and Star of Joy). If two kittens ever picked a Mewmie, it was Tairsy and Deneb.

Sadly, Altair Leilani was hit and killed by a car the next Spring. Now this is the weird part. Altair was shorthaired, and had a kind of half brown half black face. Deneb has beautiful long hair and an almost black face. However, the two were inseparable. They could have been Siamese twins. After Leilani died, Deneb started acting like her at times, She even looked like her! And at those times she would only answer to the name Leilani, not to her own name.

But what was really the strangest is that my sister and brother-in-law also saw this. There are times when they come over and they will say, "I see Tairsy is here today." It is so incredible!

The next instance involves my sweet Shadesie. She crossed the Rainbow Bridge in April of 1996, just before her 4th Birthday. She had epilepsy and it just got the best of her. She was such an incredibly courageous cat. She was also playful, and her favourite pastime was stealing the bathtub stopper and hiding it under the bath.

Well this year I got another black cat, but I didn't think she looked at all like Shadesie, other than being black like her. She never did the same things, or even went into the bathroom. Then in October my sister said "I dreamed about Shadesie last night. I wonder if she will tell Sage about the stopper."

The very next day Sage started playing in the bathtub with the stopper. Again, I was just so amazed. You'd think I would know by now." N. E. M.

Whether it is a liking for carrots by a young puppy, Tara, or an unexpected interest taken in bathroom equipment by a black cat called Sage, the behaviour of each was enough to attract the attention of our friends, and it held a clear message for them. That happened in their homes but for K L E another of our friends in the USA, even finding a kindred spirit first meant many hours spent behind the wheel of her car.

"I too, believe that cats choose their owners, only after a few experiences and my most recent with Tootie. One of my daughters and her husband at the time went to take their trash off to the dumpster in the north Georgia town they lived, which is a four hour drive from where I live. I drove up on many occasions to visit. Well, they found a starving scrawny kitten in the dumpster and my daughter felt so sorry for it. She had Michael, her husband to go into the dumpster to fetch the baby.

They took her home with them but she was never settled the whole time she was there and Robin told me she was totally out of control and needed to find her a home. She ate all her plants to pieces and angered Robin so she asked me if I would take her home with me when I got up there that weekend.

The kitten never left me alone the whole time I was there. I had to shut the door to the bedroom they bedded me down in, in order to keep her off me!

My husband never liked cats and never wanted to have one in the house. So, I took a chance on bringing her home anyway. To my surprise he liked her and didn't mind her being here. She's been here now for around four years. Also, to my surprise she never bothered any of my plants or for that matter anything else either. She is my joy and comfort and companion in the lonely times.

I know from her behaviour she had picked me before I ever got to my daughters home on that weekend, cause she greeted me like she knew me and was excited to see me. And maybe a little relieved I finally got there to bring her home. She now over rules the five Shelties I have. They don't mind her at all, she has a pick from them and he is the only one she will let rub against her or lick on her. She purrs to him and they play together. She can tolerate the others but he is her favourite one. Just wanted to share this story with you."

Whether prospective companions are arriving or returning, the close encounters with kindred spirits continue in all manners of ways, and for all kind of reasons. The close encounter related to us by SW from Stockport, England, was a return of a different but no less significant kind since it occurred when SW needed help; it was her cat, Ben, that responded. Ben had been killed in a road tragedy $2^1/_2$ years prior to the incident that SW recalls, and shortly after his death another companion sought her out and she took Lucy into her home.

"We didn't choose her, a cat sanctuary brought her to us. "Shortly afterwards Lucy got stuck up our neighbour's tall trees. I was out there for ages in the dark, talking to her - she was petrified and just would not come down. In desperation, I said "Ben, if you're there PLEASE help Lucy. Help her to come down."

At that moment SW is quite certain that her friend Ben responded to her plea. She is still, to this day, quite certain that she saw Ben, and that he was looking down at her; and attributes the sight of him to her imagination. Many would agree with her that it was in her imagination she 'saw' Ben, but she had not imagined the situation she was facing, or imagined Lucy's plight. She is in no doubt whatsoever that prior to Ben's 'appearance' Lucy would not move, yet, when her old friend Ben did appear she says that;

"Lucy slowly picked her way through the branches as if it was suddenly quite simple and jumped to the ground. Coincidence?"

Perhaps that is all that was in this instance. Many a terrified cat that has been stuck in a tree too frightened to move, has waited until the fire-brigade officer was risking life and limb reaching out to rescue them before calmly strolling down the branch, clawing its way down the trunk, marching away from the tree, and ignoring the fuss it had caused.

Co-incidence, however, can only be accepted so far and, like those we have already shared, there are many more instances to be considered that raise the same questions:

How close can we get to the kindred spirit of a pet?

How close can the kindred spirit of a pet, get to us?

Little Paws

This is a prayer for Little Paws
All up and down the land;
Driven away, no friendly voice,
Never an outstretched hand

O God of homeless things, look down
And try to ease the way
Of all the weary Little Paws
That walk the world today.

Show them a place where Little Paws
Can rest, and need not roam,
Where food and shelter, and safety from fear
Can be theirs in a loving home.

Anon.

Chapter 5

The Rescuers of Angels

Wars have been waged since time began because people on two opposing sides, or more, have considered that they alone were 'right'. Some would suggest that for anyone to be sufficiently convinced of anything they must either be the originator of the thought, or inspired by others?

Throughout history, political and religious doctrines have been just as capable of dividing people as they have been in uniting them and yet, from beneath those well worn cloaks there have come thoughts that have inspired many who do not necessarily subscribe to either politics or religion. We know from the correspondence we receive that inspiration is derived from many sources for those who share their concerns and beliefs about animals and pet/person relationships with us.

A few names continually crop up as sources of inspiration, one, St Francis of Assisi, will undoubtedly be a name that most people associate with animals no matter whether they possess religious beliefs or otherwise. Another name, William Hogarth, is far less likely to be associated with animals in the minds of many people, yet his work possibly inspired real concern for animal welfare. Both men, in fact, devoted very little time during their lives to animals, yet their influence has been enormous and both proved that while satisfaction comes from achievement, comfort comes from action.

History records that St Francis establishing at least three Franciscan Orders. His first was for Brothers, the second for Sisters, and the third was for laymen who followed

Franciscan ideals but who remained with their families outside the life of the vows of religion. However, did his work with animals create a Fourth Order that influenced others to take action on behalf of animals; others, including those for whom religion meant little or nothing?

Few would deny that there is indeed an influence today that guides people who recognize no particular religion and yet are united in their efforts to help Mother Earth survive our worst efforts to destroy Her, or help our animal companions on this planet escape the evils of human ill-treatment.

Born the son of a wealthy cloth-merchant of Assisi in 1181, Francis was originally christened John, but called Francesco because his mother was Provençal and he was born while his father was in France. As a youth he assisted his father in running his business, but in a war between Assisi and Perugia he was taken prisoner for a year and was seriously ill. Turning his back on the war he risked accusations of cowardice but his regard for the poor and for lepers was already conspicuous.

Hearing a voice which told him to 'Go and repair my house, which you see is falling down.' Francis set about the task of restoring the semi-derelict church of San Damiano of Assisi, but sold some of his father's cloth to pay for the materials, which didn't make him too popular at home. Completing his task with money he begged, he then set out on a life of creative activity and formed his Franciscan Order, gathering disciples around him and living a communal life at the Portiuncula in Assisi near a leper colony.

The first rule of the Friars Minor was founded by Francis for these Brothers of Assisi--- they were gathered from all walks of life giving up everything to follow in Francis's steps--- through poverty and humility, for the love of all God's creations.

Sharing that love of God's creations was a young girl, named Clare de Favorone, born of the Offreduccio family in Asissi in 1194. By the age of eighteen, Clare, infatuated with Francis, was so moved by his preachings that she joined him at the Portiuncula. Their spiritual love however was so pure it had to be fulfilled in the worship of God, and achieving His work, through prayer and poverty.

Renouncing all her possessions, Clare took the habit of a nun, and was formed in the religious life in Benedictine convents at Bastia and Sant Angelo di Panzo. This she followed by establishing the order of the Minoresses, or Poor Clares, brought about by her pleadings with Francis who responded by founding the Womens' order and providing Clare and her companions with a small house adjacent to the church of San Damiano. Clare became the first Abbess of the Order in 1216.

Five years later, the Secular Order, his third, was founded by Francis from practising Catholics belonging to any church body but, who remained with their families outside the life of the vows of religion. Francis had always loved the arts, music, poetry and writings, and when asked how members of the Order could contribute he replied that as long as their work was dedicated to God it would be enough.

This was the start of the Renaissance of the Middle Ages, and its influence continues to this day, with statesmen, reformers, and peace workers and many others still working under the banner of the Third Order. But, did the influence and guidance given by Francis end with this Secular Order?

During his visit to Clare at Assisi in 1224, he wrote the Canticle of the Sun. Soon afterwards he fell ill, became blind the next year, and endured agonies from primitive surgery and other medical treatment until he died in 1226, aged only forty-five. He was canonised by Gregory IX, two years after his death.

Clare had never left her convent at Assisi and was distinguished as one devoted to serving her community, practising Franciscan ideals and, especially, practising Francis' love of nature and God's animal creations. She was canonized in 1253 by Alexander IV, only two years after her death. With her passing, the seeds of the Fourth Order created by Francis, flowering first through the dedication of a kindred spirit, began to spread far beyond the confines of a convent, or even of one church, to unite peoples of conscience down the centuries.

And today --- those ideals Clare learned from Francis and shared with others, live on. Even in this complex, technological and at times, nightmare, world we live in, there are those who stop and think of his teachings. Those teachings are as alive and relevant today as they were in the 13th century. People carry forward the ideals of St Francis, not just by caring about something that is wrong but actually doing something to change it.

Those who protest about animal cruelty, and those who deal with its consequences; those who raise funds to save forests and flora; those who bring help to the world's starving peoples, the homeless and the refugees; they, and we, knowingly or otherwise all tread the path St Francis indicated. The senior citizens who share their pensions, the children giving their pocket money, the people supporting campaigns, all those who reach out to the distressed both in the natural world and the human, are all united, in mind and spirit and in practicing the ideals that Francis promoted.

Many will deny that they have any creed or religion; they have all responded to a call, and have answered with action. Others recognise that they are truly guided by their religious beliefs, and the invisible helpers of Francis; they have all responded to a call, and have answered with action. All are following the same path, in the footsteps of those who established the Fourth Order. St Francis always recognised his own limitations, and yet inspired many others to follow in his footsteps.

William Hogarth was an entirely different kettle of fish. This English painter and engraver was born in 1697 and studied his craft first under a silverplate engraver and then later at the hand of Sir James Thornhill, whose tuition fees he recovered by clandestinely marrying his daughter in 1729. Hogarth established his own reputation two years later with a series of six paintings and engravings of A Harlot's Progress which launched him on a career during which he excelled in moralizing social satires in such narrative series as *A Rake's Progress, Industry and Idleness, Gin Lane,* and the paintings of Marriage a la Mode. He showed his mettle as a campaigner, albeit with self-interest at heart probably, by taking action to secure legislation of an Engraving Copyright Act, aptly nicknamed the Hogarth Act.

His penetrating satire and inclusion of detail in every corner of his works that illustrated and emphasized the follies and vices of his times proved popular, and made him a rich man. His portrait painting had a directness that influenced his contemporaries but did not appeal to them or to the fashionable world in which he lived but these were not the works that proved to be inspirational to others either. It was not until towards the end of his career that Hogarth's works became far less humourous in content and very specific in their target.

In 1751 his new series continued to detail the things he witnessed in society and observed around him. The engravings of the Four Stages of Cruelty came as a shock to his usual patrons and, we suggest, probably signaled the start of a change in society. Hogarth described his intentions about the series in these words:

"The leading points in these, as well as in Beer Street and Gin Lane, were made as obvious as possible, in the hope that their tendency might be seen by men of the lowest rank. Neither minute accuracy of design, nor fine engraving, were deemed necessary, as the latter would render them too expensive for the persons to whom they were intended to be useful. And the fact is the passions may be more frankly expressed by a strong, bold stroke, than by the most delicate engraving.... The prints were engraved with the hope of, in some degree, correcting that barbarous treatment of animals, the very sight of which renders the streets of our metropolis so distressing to every feeling mind. If they have had this effect, and checked the progress of cruelty, I am more proud of having been the author, than I should be of having painted Raffaele's cartoons"

Hogarth, in his First Stage of Cruelty shows a street scene with the steeple of a church in the background. Tom Nero is torturing a dog that is being held by one of his accomplices. A 'merciful' young man, who is said to bear a resemblance to the young Prince who became George III, offers him a pie to persuade him to refrain from cruelty. In one picture Hogarth includes dog fighting and cock fighting among other cruelties ranging from the experiment of the two people who have launched a cat into the air from an attic window with two inflated bladders attached to its body, to a dog savaging a cat. By adding an inn sign from which the two cats are suspended he manages to indicates the collusion in cruelty of the vintner's while the only other person, in addition to the 'merciful' young man, apparently opposed to the cruelty is depicted drawing a gallows scene on a wall to suggest that such despicable actions should only have one end result for the perpetrators.

In his second print Hogarth continued to state his case clearly with Nero, now a coachman, belabouring his fallen horse, while lawyers in his crashed coach ignore all but their own discomfort. A drover is beating a sheep, a bull is baited, but at least it is throwing its tormentor into the air, and an overloaded donkey passes in front of a filled dray that is about to run over a child, because its driver is asleep.The recognition that anyone capable of cruelty to animals would similarly treat humans was carried forward by the artist in the two last prints in the series, which dealt with murder and medical research respectively. Through Hogarth's engravings, cruelty was being recognised as a sin.

Not only had Hogarth drawn attention to the scene in his last works, but by leaving more than footprints of compassion in history his action inspired others who shared his concern for animals. When William Hogarth died in 1764, a young man who was to become a Barrister and a Member of Parliament for County Galway was already ten years old.

We cannot suggest that at that age he had already been influenced by Hogarth, or even by St Francis, but was it just co-incidence that Dublin born Richard Martin was to become the man responsible for introducing the first successful legislation to protect animals and through whose efforts the Royal Society for the Prevention of Cruelty to Animals was formed?

Through Richard Martin's work, cruelty was to be recognised as a crime. His Bill, which received Royal Assent on 22nd July 1822, was the first legislation of its kind and was intended to; ".... *prevent the cruel and improper treatment of cattle, that if any person or persons having the charge care or custody of any horse, mare, gelding, mule, and ass, cow, ox, heifer, steer, sheep or other cattle, the property of any other person or persons, shall wantonly beat, abuse or ill-treat any such animal, such individuals shall be brought before a justice of the peace or other administrator.*"

The penalty for such crimes against animals was fixed as a fine of no less than ten shillings (50p) and not exceeding £5, or imprisonment for not more than two months. Action had brought results for the politician and comfort to those who were inspired to go further.

The Rev. Arthur Broome, Mr T. Fowell Buxton MP, Mr William Wilberforce MP, and many others are often offered by our friends as people whose work inspired them, our present day animal protectors, rescuers, and voluntary workers. With the passing of the Animal Protection Act, the principal that animals had rights was recognised, and was enshrined in law, giving added impetus to those who had long supported the cause.

An organisation had been formed to promote the need for animal protection well over a decade earlier, in October 1809. Citizens of Liverpool had then attempted to establish a 'Society for the Suppression and Prevention of Wanton Cruelty to Animals' but their efforts appear to have swiftly foundered since records of only two meetings of the supporters group held around that time have been found.

In London, after Richard Martin saw his Bill succeed in 1822, the Rev Arthur Broome set out to form a society for animal protection. The vicar, whose parish was that of St Mary's Bromley St Leonard, now the London parish of Bromley-by-Bow, found little support given to his efforts but this did not dissuade him from vigorously continuing to promote his ideals.

In a society where life was cheap, crime was a way of life, and prison was but a lodging place for many on their way to the gallows, the proposition that animals needed protection was not one that was received with enthusiasm. It was hardly a topic worthy of being considered at all by most people, but the vicar, however, was a passionate believer in animal welfare, and was persistent in promoting that cause.

In 1824 he believed the time was right for a public meeting to be called to consider the need for the formation of a national body which could take up the gauntlet and continue the work. The meeting, it was decided, was to be held in the rather appropriately named Old Slaughter's Coffee House, in St Martin's Lane, London, and publicised as being held "for the purpose of preventing cruelty to animals." Held on June 16th, that public gathering has since become recognised as the inaugural meeting of what became the first national animal protection society in the world, the Society for the Prevention of Cruelty to Animals; and The Rev. Arthur Broome was no longer without influential supporters.

Mr T. Fowell Buxton MP chaired the meeting during which the Rev. Broome was appointed the society's first Honourary Secretary. Among the society's founder members present that day were Mr Richard Martin MP, Mr William Wilberforce MP, Sir Jas. Mackintosh MP, Mr A. Warre MP, and Mr Lewis Gompertz, the man who was to succeed Arthur Broome as Secretary in 1828. With the society established on a firm foundation, Broome gave up his ecclesiastical 'living' to devote his attention to its animal welfare work and the two committees that were set up. One committee provided public relations support to the society by overseeing the publication of tracts, sermons, and other material that would influence public opinion.

Another committee undertook to adopt and impose measures for inspecting London's markets, streets, and slaughterhouses, and to watch carefully the conduct of coachmen and others whose occupations were associated with the use, and oft-times abuse, of animals. Hogarth's 'coachman' in his cruelty series was obviously still very much in evidence. A little over a year later, however, the fledgling SPCA was in financial difficulties and Broome was imprisoned because of its debts.

Lewis Gompertz and Richard Martin came to his rescue with money enough to ensure his release, and Broome repaid them by dedicating the rest of his life to ensuring the future of the society by unstintingly pursuing the then unpopular cause of animal protection. His courageous work ensured not only the future of the SPCA but, by its very existence, provided others around the world with an example to follow.

In 1840, three years after the death of its first Honourary Secretary and most prominent founder member, honour and recognition was given to the society, when 'Royal' was added to its title. Over a century and a half later, the work that Arthur Broome considered essential for the well being of animals and necessary for the salvation of man, continues to be essential and necessary in each case today.

Over a century and half later a new millennium dawns on age where Hogarth's engravings would need little modification to become relevant to our times. He might have needed to place some of the activities behind closed laboratory doors but, just as he highlighted the improbable experiment of a bladder propelled cat ascending into the sky, should we not remind ourselves of how long it is since we propelled a dog into space?

M D L from London reminded us recently that Matthew Fox once said, "*Animals don't need avatars to teach them how to be animals, only humans need to be taught to be human. My dog knew perfectly well how to be a dog, while most of us don't know how to be human.*"

She also added that, "*unconditional love, to name one thing, comes much more easily to animals than to people.*" Like many others she finds her inspiration from sources that some may find difficult to understand while, obviously, heading in the same direction.

She disputes the anthropocentric idea that animals eventually reincarnate as human beings, considering this is to be an arrogant suggestions, and obviously inaccurate, since in some ways animals are superior to humans. She puts the idea that every species is on its own path of spiritual advancement - a path unique to itself, not readily comprehensible to human beings.

"As each human being eventually returns to the Source (or Monad) of all human life, so each species has its own Source to which each member eventually returns. I realise that I am disputing many respected mystics - but in the late 19th century when most of these mystics were writing, Darwinism was all the fad and channelled information (even, admittedly, mine) is always coloured by the prejudices of the channel. But the paradigm shift and the animal rights movement have humbled human beings somewhat, so perhaps now is the time for this information to come out.

I believe that the animal-headed gods of the ancients (and the full animal gods of the native Americans and Australian aboriginal) were our ancestors' way of honouring the Sources of the animals who served them well. Therefore whenever I lose a cat, I pray for its soul to the cat goddess Bast. For lost dogs, I pray to Anubis and for horses to the horse goddess Epona.

Another piece of channelled information: whenever a species becomes extinct (except of course through man's interference) what happens is that the Monad itself is evolving - moving on to a higher plane of existence from the transpersonal to the universal. This is primarily why we are now losing the big cats: the lion goddess Sekhmet is evolving (though they won't all be gone for a few hundred years more). This also explains why the dinosaurs disappeared: their Monad evolved from the transpersonal to the universal. In 100 million years it should have!"

Others express their own, and often differing opinions, just as opinions have differed down the centuries yet, the progress of the rescuers of animals and of those concerned with animal welfare in the physical or spiritual sense, has always been, albeit slowly, forward progress.

J R B who comes from Wales set her ideas forth quite clearly, after detailing a strange experience of some years ago when the black cat her family had didn't appear, but let her know quite clearly, all day while she was at school, that he had died that day.

"Words like black, last, depressing, etc kept cropping up in conversations all day, even the weather was depressing, thick fog, and damp mist all day. When I got back from school, my mum said "I'm sorry, but Pinckie died today! I said I know, and told her how I knew. It was as if Pinckie was trying to break the news to me gently, himself.

We have had many cats since then, but so far he is the only one, who we've had an encounter with. I often wonder why.

Did you ever read about the couple in the newspaper, who had to have their cat put down? They were so upset their R.C. priest came to see them after the vet certified that it had gone. They gave it its last night with candles around its box, and a rosary. When the couple went down stairs the next morning, the husband thought it funny as there were noises, coming from the box, the man lifted the lid of the box to find his cat had come back to life, and was behaving in a very kittenish fashion.

I also wrote to the society for companion animal studies and one of its members had this to say to me - "I am a Christian and believe that there is an after-life for animals and that we will all meet again - I do not believe in spiritualism but I have a very strong faith in God and many Christians feel as I do

about after-life for animals. There are references in the Bible to this, one is in Isaiah 11 - 6 This is a description of what it will be like when the peace of God is fully known when the animals will live in harmony with each other and with all of the human race.

Pope John Paul II on 19th January 1990 said "*Animals possess a soul and men must love and feel solidarity with our smaller brethren------- Animals are as near to God as men are*"

The Archdeacon of Chesterfield, in an article in Derby Cathedral Notes and Comments writes:- St Paul looks forward to the time when " creation itself will be set free from its bondage to decay and obtain the glorious liberty of the children of God" *Romans 8*. He speaks of the whole of creation groaning in the travail together, which suggests that Redemption has more than human or even earthly limits.

W. H. Elliot, a former Dean of St Paul's, hoped that when he got to Heaven he would feel a familiar wet nose pushing into his hand.

The Reverend Professor Andrew Linzey has written in a book "*Animal Theology*" and he states "I affirm the hope of the world to come for all living creatures. I will trust in the redeeming power of God's love to transform the universe"

I ought to say no-one can positively prove that there is an after-life for humans but if there is then there should be one for animals too because God loves everything that he has made. There are many men and women in the church in high positions who believe that there is an after-life for animals. Another Bible reference is Ephesians I.

So much information crammed into one letter, but didn't Hogarth manage to cram a great deal of information into one picture? P W K had two little Yorkshire Terriers, Penny and Cindy, who came to her as pups. She says that she was privileged to have them as very, very loved members of her family for twelve years.

Cindy and Penny were very close and loved each other dearly and PWK felt sure that they are now both with her mother, in Spirit, but thought that in adding that opinion it was a digression from her main points. We'll deal with the 'digression' after considering those main points.

"When Cindy was about ten years old she developed epilepsy and had fits all the time - she was put on tablets and although the fits were controlled, they never went away. Meanwhile Penny also became ill and was diagnosed as diabetic but not before she went blind. Because she was such a happy little dog, always chasing things, her blindness hit her terribly and I don't think she could cope with it, despite our love and my healing sessions, and about a month after her blindness

*became complete, she passed on over 29th January 1988. My
little Cindy missed her badly and gradually went into a
decline and passed over a few months later on 9th June 1988.*

*I have been aware of their presence since then, especially when
I feel 'down' they rush around the house as they always did
and there have been many occasions when I have had to stop
because I felt or 'sensed' that one or the other was lying across
my path. My husband who is an avid sceptic has admitted
that he too has seen them. I sat in development circles for
many, many years and have no doubt that they live on in the
Spirit world.*

*Finally, I must pen the most astonishing thing of all. When we
had our little dogs we lived on the very busy Long Lane in
Middlesex which linked the A40 with the Uxbridge road and,
as you can imagine the traffic non-stop all night but before
each little dog died an owl hooted outside the house for three
nights each time and after each dog had passed. I never heard
it again, and I was the only one who heard the owl. I am
convinced that the owl came to take them over.*

As for the, 'digression', wasn't the whole point about P W K's
letter about spiritual guidance and understanding, and
sharing with us, all of us, the attempts made to help her pet-
companions? Did we not learn that even, as she put it, 'an
avid sceptic' admitted to an experience that, if he had only
heard about from someone else, would simply not have
believed in?

We would simply suggest that an opinion held, expressed, and
considered is more likely to influence others than an opinion
held and never expressed. A R L from Merseyside had a
Burmese cat named Rampa, who died last year at the age of
12. Rampa was one of several cats she shared her life with,
and was the one with whom she knew she had a very special
and close relationship.

"About six weeks or so after his death, I was lying in bed in the state between sleep and full consciousness. I know I was awake and that this was not a dream. I felt something jump onto my bed, although I was alone in the house and with no other animals. The sensation was familiar to me as when a cat jumps onto a bed.

I could not see anything but was aware that the 'something' on the bed was walking towards me. I felt very strongly that it was my cat Rampa. He came right up to me and pushed his nose against my face, which I felt as if a live cat was actually doing this. I felt that he was saying 'goodbye' to me.

A few weeks later a similar experience occurred, although he did not push his nose against me. Nothing has happened since."

C R S from Kent has always loved cats and feels that she has been lucky to have them around her all her life.

"I had a real character called Julie in my teens and when I married, she came to live with us, aged 14. At 19 she died, and for a long time after, I felt her jump on my bed and curl up at my feet. Although I missed her a lot, I found this very comforting as if she was still there although I could not see her.

Nine years ago I was given a dark tortoiseshell cat called Tansy. She was so much like Julie in temperament that I often found it unnerving. We loved her dearly and six months before she was killed on the road we got a ginger tom called Oscar. She didn't like him very much although she did get used to him.

About three months after her death I went to see a psychic and I was not thinking of Tansy at all that day. She held a silver bracelet, which I always wear and immediately said she had a strong link with a dark female cat. I had gone to her because I had been very troubled by a relationship and was unsure of my future. As much as I missed my Tansy, I most definitely was not thinking about her that day. Anyway, the psychic said the link was very strong indeed and told me that the cat told her a lot about me and that I was a lovely person (which made me cry) and that we had shared other lifetimes before and that she was still with me.

I was very shaken by this and emotional as you can imagine, I'm sure. She went on to other aspects of my life and about 20 minutes later she said, "Your cat just wants you to know that the tom you've got now will always be a pest and although you are trying to love him, he'll never replace her." I just burst out laughing - that was so typical of her - I could just hear her saying it. I've never been one for photos around the house but I have a picture of her on the fireplace and I do indeed feel she is still around. And yes, I am trying to love Oscar although he is fond of biting, it's sometimes hard!"

D S S who lives in Hertfordshire, also had a much-loved cat, Cindy, and also lost her friend a few years ago.

"When she died, aged 18, I was so distraught that I spent the following three days crying my eyes out! However, the following morning just as I was waking up, imagine how amazed and delighted I was to 'feel' her curled up in my arms! She was washing herself, purring very loudly and obviously in the best of health!

The following two mornings, again just as I was waking, I 'felt' her sitting on my shoulder (as she often used to) and again she was purring loudly! She never made contact with me again but that was enough to convince me (a former sceptic) that there was indeed a happy afterlife - at least for cats! I hope my story may be of some comfort to any readers who've experienced the devastation that losing a much-loved cat can bring.

PS. A year later I visited the Wood Green Animal Shelter and adopted two tortoiseshell sisters, Emma and Purdy, whom I love dearly."

The sceptic was converted it seems, and not only converted to a belief she would not have considered some years ago, but she also benefited from a visit to an Animal Shelter. Could it possibly be that the shelter might not even have come into existence if others hadn't expressed their opinion in the past?

JW lives and works in the British West Indies, A few years ago she and her husband were in England visiting relatives. For the visitors this meant a few days here, a few days there, just to see everyone they could. Their time together was short and precious but two of the relatives were people who took an interest in the protection of cats, and a new cattery had recently been opened near to their home. They'd taken an interest in it and when the visitors said they'd also like to see what a cattery was all about, they arranged to visit it. The lady in charge was only too willing to talk about her work with cats that had been cruelly abused, the work of societies like the Cats Protection League, the PDSA, and RSPCA. The visitors were clearly moved by seeing the cats being treated with kindness, gradually recovering their health, and beginning to trust humans.

Minutes turned into hours but the visitors eventually left the cattery.

Some months later the relatives received a letter from JW saying that she had found an animal rescue organisation on the island on which she lived and that she was now helping out there every Saturday. That was a few years ago now and the Saturday work with animals still continues.

There is, we suggest, a thread running all through the events and incidents we have shared in this section. No matter which route was followed, the religious influence of St Francis, the artistic route of William Hogarth, the political route of Richard Martin, the route through the Spirit world, or the route through any of the organisations that have arisen to serve the needs of animals, the end result is similar. When it comes to understanding and helping our pet-companions, or caring for animals in any way, we will come to learn, like those we have mentioned, and many more beside, that satisfaction does comes from achievement, and that great comfort comes from action.

The Voice of the Voiceless
We are the voice of the voiceless,
Through us the dumb shall speak
'Til the dead world's ear can be made to hear
The cry of the wordless weak.

From street, ice floe and lab. cage,
From stable, field or zoo,
The wail of our tortured kin proclaims
The sins that the mighty do.

The same force formed the sparrow
That fashioned man, the king.
The God of the whole gave a spark of soul
To furred and feathered thing

And we are our brother's keeper
And we will fight his fight,
And speak the word for beast and bird
'Til the world shall set things right.

Anon.

Chapter 6

Trust and Loyalty Know No Barriers; Physical or Spiritual

Even when its suffering seems to have no end, the ill-treated animal will still show trust in the human that cruelly abuses them. When kindness and consideration replaces ill-treatment, the trust, devotion, and loyalty that many of God's creatures will lavish upon a rescuer is more than just a reward, it is a beacon of love kindled in the animal kingdom that can bring warmth to humanity.

Most of us are protected from the real, first-hand, knowledge of just how cruel a human can be to an animal. The RSPCA letters asking us for our help may shake our complacency every now and then and, conscience stricken, we send off a donation. This we will consider in another chapter while we consider here the trust and loyalty that can exist not only between pet and person, but also between animals alone.

In London, S A C had a long established pet/person companionship that began long before she married and, sadly, ended when her lovely black cat died at the age of $17\frac{1}{2}$ years from kidney failure. Or was that the end of the relationship? For several months afterwards S A C felt that her friend was still 'with' her, but eventually came to realize that others also sensed that he was still there.

"I always talk to any cat I meet and several of these would suddenly stare at a point by my feet where I assume he must have been sitting. I could see Nothing! Being Christian, I have never had any problems with the concept of life after death and cannot see why it should be any different for cats than for humans as cats too have very distinct personalities."

The brief experience might have influenced S A C's belief, and then been forgotten, had it not been for other events that were to illustrate loyalties that were seemingly not confined to one world.

"Last year we lost our beloved Toby after some months of illness, though it was a wasp bite that did for him. He did not have the strength to fight the poison and had to be put to sleep to stop him suffering further. We buried him in the garden next to his best friend who had died at the end of 1991.

A few days later, I noticed Felix, another of our mob, staring at the spot where they were buried. Then his gaze moved to the garden next door and followed 'something' up and down the path. He even sat up on his haunches to get a better view of whatever was going on. Neither my husband nor I could see anything, so we rather thought that the two old friends must be re-enacting their famous double-act. Chasing and play-fighting were their favourite pastimes together and they had been inseparable since Toby had brought Fattypuss home to live with us. He was a stray, unclaimed, and at least part Burmese.

Toby had grieved for many months after he lost his friend, so we think they were making up for lost time. This went on for several days with Felix also staring at and also backing away from the place in the kitchen where Toby ate. Though we were sad this all helped to lift the gloom. Toby was 15.

Our conviction that Felix sees ghosts was reinforced earlier this year when our 'dumb blond' Topsy died and was buried in a different part of the garden.

A day or two later, Felix rushed in through the cat-flap as though pursued by demons, making for the front window ledge. Eventually he crept into the conservatory and sat staring at the spot where Topsy was buried. This time it did not last as long. Topsy did not like other cats getting too close to her, so we think she may have chased him off when he inadvertently 'walked on her grave'!

This all reminded us that when Felix first came to live with us (another unclaimed stray) just after Fattypuss had died, he was obsessed with the cupboard under the stairs where Fattypuss used to often sit. Both cats would make quite a fuss if the door was closed. Felix does not try to get in there nowadays. Apart from ghost cats as such, there is the case of 'doubles' as described in the article. (Your Cat magazine, Dec. 1997.) We've experienced that too.

Soon after Toby died, we had to take another of our cats to the vet's. At the reception desk was the picture of a cat very much like Toby and in need of a new home. Toby was black and white with a 'moustache' rather than the more usual white blaze. This cat also had one but a slightly different shape. I remarked to the receptionist that when my husband (who was parking the car) saw the photo he would want the cat; he had been particularly fond of Toby. She said we could meet the cat, Stanley as he was called, when we had seen the vet. We did and it was love at first sight, so he came to join us the very next day.

Stanley fitted straight into Toby's place with us and the other cats as his character as well as his looks was almost the same. The main reason that no-one else had snapped him up we think is that he is blind in one eye, probably from fighting as he was a full tom when the vet took him in. He is not the same as Toby - but does a lot of things in the same way and on the same level. Some people think it odd that we are not upset being daily reminded of Toby but we actually find it comforting especially after our earlier experiences with Felix and the ghosts."

At almost the same time that S A C was writing to us another letter arrived from J G who lives in Lancashire, had also read the magazine article, and included details of another incident about 'doubles', among other things.

"A strange thing happened to me just before reading your article in December's Your Cat. I had spent the evening on my computer, most of the time working on a photograph of my late, much- lamented Jenny, trying to print out a good quality enlargement. I then went downstairs and picked up a book to read, but the heading "Ghostly Tales" on the newly-arrived and as-yet unopened Your Cat magazine lying beside me caught my eye. As I have my own ghostly cat tale to tell, I picked up the magazine and opened it at random to flick through for the article. The magazine fell open at page 27, a completely unrelated article to the one I was searching for, but imagine my surprise to be confronted with a photograph which was almost a duplicate of the one I had been working on all evening !

Jenny was born on or around 7th September 1979, the day my husband Phil and I married, and she was our first 'marital' cat, clearly born to be with us. She loved both of us very deeply, although she never cared for other people and was regarded as stand-offish, even downright unfriendly, by our friends and family.

No-one believed that she was the most affectionate cat, that she slept every night between us on the pillows, that she would gently remove our spectacles with her teeth and nose in order to get closer for a kiss. Her lifelong companion, tabby Maxie, contracted cancer early in 1994 at the age of 14. She gave up on life very quickly, retreating to the bathroom where she was free of both people and other cats. It was obvious that having her put to sleep was the kindest thing to do, even though it broke our hearts.

When Jenny's jaw began to twist a year later, we thought it was the result of a struggle with the vet during a tooth-cleaning session. She had not been anaesthetized because she had suffered with chronic kidney-disease for several years. We were devastated when the vet's x-ray revealed bone-cancer, and she was given a matter of weeks to live. Naturally, we expected her to react to the pain in the same way that Maxie had. We, however, underestimated Jenny's love of life.

Although her jaw twisted further and further backwards, restricting her to a liquidized diet, and her fur became progressively more matted and impossible to groom, Jenny refused to give up on life. She was first in the queue at mealtimes, as she had always been, remaining very much the top cat despite her frail body. The phrase 'indomitable spirit' sums her up completely. This made it very hard to make a decision about the 'right' time to end it all for her. Eventually, however, her quiet periods of just staring into space increased and we made the appointment with the vet that we dreaded so much.

When the time came to put her in the cat-basket for the last time, she climbed slowly up to the top of the armchair in the bay window, looked out for a while at the view of the heath in front of our then-home, and came down again, rubbed around our legs, and walked into the basket of her own accord. If ever a cat has indicated that it was time to move on, it was Jenny.

About a month later I had a strange dream. I was walking up a spiral staircase when I met Jenny at the half-way point. Her jaw was back to normal and her fur no longer matted. When I stroked her, I could feel that she was again the elderly cat that she had been before the cancer. I woke up overjoyed and told my husband "Jenny is getting better."

About two months after that incident, we were in Portugal on holiday. I woke up on the first morning to find Jenny sitting in her accustomed position in between us on the pillows, purring softly and looking down at me with love in her huge golden eyes. I stroked her and was pleased to find that her coat was back to its very best condition. She was a magnificent, beautiful, long-haired cat in her prime once more. She was gone in the blink of an eye, leaving me feeling very happy. My husband woke up moments later and was not at all surprised by my story. Like me, he had never ceased to 'feel' her presence."

S A C was not a lady who was worried by the paranormal or the unusual in any way. She had spent the first thirteen years of her life in what was reputed to be a haunted house, so mysterious sightings or ghostly apparitions did not surprise or frighten her. She was quite used to living with the sound of footsteps upstairs, when she knew without doubt that no-one else was in the house. Doors opening of their own accord failed to draw more response than a muttered 'ttchh' on sharply exhaled breath when she closed it again. It never occurred to her that other families did not have a parlour like hers, cold and eerie and used only to store the milk. There were no refrigerators in her younger days. The stairs in the house frightened her though. Before she was born her father had blocked up a glass panel in the stairs door, which looked out into the living room, apparently because his late grandmother used to peer through it and frighten everybody.

Anyone who grows up in or is used to living in an old house or cottage, one that others might shy away from and consider 'weird' or 'spooky', will have probably enjoyed many years occupying property in which experience is likely to have shown them that ninety percent of all 'ghostly' happenings have a very down-to-earth cause. If they are extremely fortunate they will have enjoyed learning to live with those who cause the other ten-percent of the 'happenings'. S A C could recall only one ghostly cat incident, and that happened one Boxing Day just after her eighth birthday.

"One of our two cats, a little ginger-and-white tom called Timmy, had been run over and killed in the road the day before - completely ruining my Christmas. When I told my friend next door but one about this on Boxing Day, his father gave me a strange look. Our ginger and white cat, he said, had been sitting on his shed roof when he went out for coal late on Christmas night - hours after he had been killed."

Christmas day was obviously not a joyful one for S A C that year but did her little ginger-and-white tom linger near its young friend long enough to ensure that she, to whom it was loyal, would come to at least hear of its presence after the accident? Years later, the area was redeveloped and her house, along with its three neighbours, was condemned.

"We heard from neighbours that the local children were having great fun playing in the empty houses - except ours, which they refused to enter. Getting back to Jenny, it is a great comfort to me to think that she is always around, even though I haven't really seen her again. I have, more than once, seen a shadowy long-haired black cat moving around in front of me and thought it was Zippy, our long-haired black-and-white, only to discover that he is asleep behind me.

When we go away on holiday, I tell myself that we are not really leaving the cats behind. The five living ones may have to stay at home, but Jenny and Maxie can be with us anywhere in the world. There are no quarantine restrictions where they go.

Sitting on top of a shed roof to ensure that the news of a walk across the Rainbow Bridge is spread is one way of doing things and, on this occasion, independent confirmation of the presence of the cat on the shed probably stemmed more than just a few tears from being shed by a heart-broken young girl; even if she didn't understand why at the time.

Communication can come in all sorts of unusual forms though and from what she told us, a lady from Devon, England, might have encountered one of the world's most communicative cats after acquiring a one year old, 'She' from the Cats Protection League.

Actually, P M L said that the young lady had acquired her, and had insisted on being taken home. The newcomer, Sue, was a very friendly animal who was soon, 'at home' in the entire district, and would greet all new neighbours as soon as they moved in. She would even answer the door if the bell rang and P M L was in the garden, greet the visitor and keep them entertained until relief arrived in the shape of a flurried gardener.

Unfortunately, Sue lost an eye in an accident, and a few years later, was killed in a weekend road accident in March in which, probably, she did not see the vehicle approaching on her blind side.

"Everyone was very upset about this and on the Sunday morning - 10a.m. I had a phone call from my cousins in Sydney (Australia) asking if I was alright. This call was entirely out of the blue - they keep cats as well."

Obviously, relatives do keep in touch with each other, even when they live on opposite sides of the world and that call might have been forgotten. However, P M L was to have an unfortunate reason for remembering it.

"On 5th July my Persian cat Reginald died at the Vets from a fit, due to age - he was a stray but we believe he must have been quite old. On the 6th July, in the evening, I had another call from my cousins asking if I was alright; also out of the blue. One of my neighbours is sure Sue is on a satellite between Exeter and Sydney.

A few weeks ago she asked if I had heard from my cousins lately I said 'No' so she said laughingly - "Sue get on your Satellite Dish" - the next day I had a call from them. Just after Sue (short for Susannah) had died I visited a Clairvoyant who told me I had a lot of happy animal spirits around me and in particular she asked me if I had lost a very small white puppy lately. I said I had never owned a dog and then told her about my experience with the Australian phone calls - I happened to mention that Susannah was white with black markings and then she immediately said it must have been her she could see. She said she is always near me with the other cat spirits around about, but the 'white' animal was the nearest at that time.

I am sure that Sue somehow got in touch with my Australian cousins on each occasion of their phone calls and asked them to call me. I am very close to those cousins and often visit them.

PS. Sue was a throwback to a Siamese - would this have anything to do with her mental powers?"

Unfortunately, not being experts on Siamese cats, nor having had the pleasure of knowing Sue, we cannot even begin to answer the question but P M L's letter did cause us some concern. Look back for the full context but you may recall that after Sue died P M L visited a Clairvoyant who told her that she had a lot of happy animal spirits around her, and particularly asked if she had lost a very small white puppy lately. P M L said that she had never owned a dog but happened to mention that Sue had been white, with black markings. The clairvoyant immediately said it must have been Sue she could see.

Now, we certainly appreciate that a helping hand at the time of the loss of a beloved pet is beneficial but, if a clairvoyant cannot distinguish between a cat and a dog, we feel bound to inquire, 'who is benefiting from what?'

Trust is a fragile thing and while working together on this book, albeit separated by several counties, Evelyn and I were both conscious of the trust that others put in us. From the outset we were aware that when people were providing us with their very private thoughts, their experiences, their beliefs, they were also trusting us to find the ways and words to share those treasures with others.

During our own lives we had both experienced events, and losses, that were similar to those described in correspondence received from people around the world. Our own experiences, and mutual belief in an after life, had provided us with the foundation for working together on a project that we both hoped others might find helpful, even comforting perhaps. It also provided us with the opportunity to learn.

When Evelyn's cat, Tippi, was taken ill, and the end was approaching, Evelyn telephoned me at times, not to discuss our work, just to talk. We both knew that the time was coming when Tippi would need the help of her devoted human friend; loving help, that Evelyn would find it very difficult indeed to provide; as all of us do when faced with the situation.

We soon learn that friendship does not come unaccompanied, with it always comes responsibility. Many who have more than once found themselves facing up to taking their beloved pet to the veterinarian for the final time know that only too well; but it never makes decision taking any easier.

How do you make the decision to end a life that means so much to you? With an understanding of true love, loyalty, and trust, is possibly the answer.

With a desire to relieve pain and suffering as, perhaps, the guide to understanding. Evelyn, and her husband Bert, took Tippi to the veterinary surgery one Wednesday, and parted from their friend. Each grieved the sad loss of their personal friend and, not unexpectedly, the experience had a particularly demoralising effect on Evelyn. An effect that depressingly continued through succeeding days. Tippi was missed a great deal.

Their special cat that had grown in beauty, lived with them in valued friendship but, when first attracting the couple's attention at the animal sanctuary, had been a cat considered by the staff to be "un-home-able." They had believed that, scarred as she was by her early ill treatment, this cautious creature was one that definitely, "will not to trust any human being again." The Warden had little doubt that the cat was beyond any help. It had been so badly treated since kittenhood that it trusted no-one; and it showed its feelings with claw drawn intensity.

Evelyn had regard for the claws, and heard yet more words, important words, her own words. 'Just let me try' were the words she had uttered; and Tippi had selected her home.

In the quiet of the house those words again came clearly, across the years, to Evelyn. Yet in reality the years had already passed with much happiness in them, brought about by that furry companion who had seemed to understand Evelyn's plea to the Warden of, "just let me try." Now their home seemed empty and Tippi's absence made each hour seem as long as two and even the house itself appeared to be aware that one of its resident was missing. Loneliness crept into the home where Tippi had so recently provided companionship. The kitchen provided cold comfort for the couple each morning when there was no Tippi present to share the start of the day with.

Bert was keenly aware of Evelyn's depressed state and didn't waste much time when he went shopping in the nearby town, just two days after taking Tippi to the veterinarian there. He was in town just long enough though for a friend to notice his presence. Double yellow lines stopped that friend from parking her car and going across to speak to him, so she drove home. It was later that she resolved to phone Evelyn.

When the call came, Evelyn answered the phone and was surprised to hear her friend, Kate, asking if Kitty was alright. "Kitty" was the convenient identification that Kate bestowed upon all of the cats possessed by people she knew. Let us admit it, few of us can remember the names of every pet owned by our friends and acquaintances. Somehow, this adoption of the singular yet unspecific word, 'kitty,' made Kate's conversations with anyone and everyone relate quite acceptably to whichever cat she was inquiring about. However, this particular conversation continued apace with the unexpected caller explaining that after seeing Bert, she had returned home but, much later, felt that it was necessary to speak to Evelyn about a recent incident.

During the flow of the conversation Evelyn learned that her

friend had driven into town a few days earlier to go shopping. After completing the task she returned to the car-park where she found a beautiful orange and black cat strolling around her car. Evelyn's depression lifted immediately as Kate went on to describe the cat and the encounter in greater detail. Although the cat seemed vaguely familiar to her, Kate couldn't place it properly, yet she was certain that it had been waiting there, just for her, waiting until she returned to her car. "Without any doubt," Kate was saying, "the cat demanded my attention the moment I appeared, and the thing is," she continued, "when I reached down to stroke this gorgeous creature, my hand went straight through her. She was there in Spirit only, my dear, and while I was pleased to experience the encounter, I could see no reason for my being favoured by a cat returning from the other side."

Evelyn knew very well that Kate was an accomplished clairvoyant and that she had been listening to her describing Tippi, and a meeting with her that had taken place two days after Tippi died.

Kate's call worked wonders.The knowledge that Tippi had passed through to the Spirit world, and was now safe and free from pain, was the tonic that Evelyn needed; and Bert too for that matter. Their world suddenly seemed brighter again; except for one question. Evelyn wondered why Tippi had chosen not to return to her.

When she called me and discussed this, it seemed to me that at the time of Kate's encounter, Evelyn herself had probably been the last person Tippi could have communicated with. My friend, distressed at the death of her cat and feeling guilty for the part she had so reluctantly played in it, had taken refuge behind a barrier that Tippi could not bypass. The cat, however, had every intention of confirming her safe passage to the Spirit world, and chose Kate as the person through whom she could pass the information on.

Despite Evelyn's own abilities and beliefs, she had, I believe, created an emotional barrier of which she was unaware; and, since it was a new experience, she was unable to understand her own situation. Able as she is, Kate, at that time, was like many who 'see' the other world, without understanding why. Their responsibility, and a privilege it is, is to find the people to whom the things they witness will hold a meaning.

Was it then, just by accident that Bert went shopping and was briefly seen by Kate? We don't think so. Evelyn not only gained comfort from the news she received from Kate, she also gained knowledge from her experience that she can share with others. During the writing period of this book there have been a number of occasions when items for inclusion seemed to suddenly present themselves; for, perhaps, good reason.

One January evening I was sitting at home with Ursula, watching the TV news, when our viewing was interrupted by someone knocking at the door. A beaming smile on the hairy

face of a dear friend greeted me across the threshold, a friend whom we would have expected to be at his home in France, instead of roaming Devon's winter moorlands. As with any true friendship, the time since our last meeting and the present disappeared in an instant and with the clasp of outstretched hands.

Our time together was to be brief though, and almost instantly over. In precious minutes, within an hour, we talked of our families, other friends, and put the world to rights; but did not discuss this work. Then came some sad but, for me, thought provoking news.

Animals are as much a companion to our friend in his life, as food is companion to drink; they naturally go together. It was obviously distressing for him when he told us of the death of Brodie, one of his dogs. Both Ursula and I had known the great lolloping hound that, spread out across a three-seater settee, had left hardly enough room for a human so it was sad to hear of the hit-and-run road incident that robbed the hound of his ability to even walk away from the country crossroad where it had occurred. Days of veterinarian attention could not overcome the damage sustained by the dog and our friend's eyes blinked rather more rapidly than normal when he told us of the final chapter of its life.

Resigned to allowing the pet to pass over in his own time, in as comfortable a manner as could be provided our friend and his wife were surprised to find many other dogs from round the country area converging on their property.

Some of those arriving on their doorstep they recognised as pets, or working dogs, owned by neighbours, or local farmers. Others, among what became a procession of dogs, were unknown to them. All of them, however, appeared to be known to the injured animal that responded to every sniff and paw-touch that came his way.

"It was, without any doubt," our friend confided, *"the final visit of lifetime friends, to another whose life-time was closing."*

Brodie was the kind of dog that made an impression on anyone he encountered. His size belied his gentleness, his bulk concealed a loyal friend.

Another of our friends, R B, from Surrey, once wrote a message to his friend Mickey and kindly agreed that we could use it here; for all the Mickeys and Brodies who mean so much to so many.

"I know you won't be able to read these words, as such, because chaps like you never needed to read, as all that you perceived was through what we humans call "intuition", and with that particular quality you (and, indeed, all pets like you) could easily tell what we were thinking and knew everything that was going on; so you see, you weren't just "a dog" but very much a person and we loved and respected you as one of the family.

It is just one reason why all of us are going to miss you so much, not to mention all the ladies and chaps here at Burrows Lea. If you weren't in one office cadging a biscuit, you were certainly in another sharing a lunch-time sandwich; and as for those Saturday occasions, remember how you always seemed to know in advance when we were holding a day seminar here, or due to entertain a party from one of the Churches?

From about 9 o'clock in the morning you would be sitting in the hall with your eyes fixed on the front door waiting for all your friends to arrive, knowing that one glance from those large black eyes of yours would have them eating out of your hand - or rather, I should say, it was precisely the other way round, for what you contrived to do on these occasions was to go from group to group at tea time, sit there right in front of them whilst they were having their cakes and biscuits, or just stare solidly at them until finally they could resist you no longer: and so it became a biscuit here, a piece of cake there, and so on and on, until you were full - and how full you used to get!

However, you made your presence felt in that very appealing way of yours and over the years you made hundreds of friends, a privilege not enjoyed by a lot of dogs, I might add. Do you remember our regular Sunday morning wrestling matches? You would be waiting for me in the corner of the dining room and I would be waiting for you in the opposite corner in my dressing gown and pyjamas crouched on all fours. We would eye each other warily and then there would be some uncanny signal, and you would charge. For the next second there was chaos as we rolled over and over, you barking fiercely and me trying to avoid those razor teeth as I pushed you and shoved you and rolled you over and over. How you loved it all!

One morning - and I didn't tell you about this - I misjudged your snapping jaws and you caught me at the base of my thumb. I conceded a quick victory to you as I rushed to the kitchen sink to turn the cold tap on the gash to stop it bleeding. Today, I look fondly at the fine white line of a scar that will always remind me of you and of our boisterous wrestling matches.

Do you remember the row we had coming back from one of our long walks in Hurtwood Forest? Well, it wasn't exactly a row, but I certainly got your message from those big sort of cartoon balloons that would appear spasmodically just over your head. It was on a very hot Sunday afternoon in summer when we went up to the forest for our usual stroll and I decided to come back a different way. I got us both hopelessly lost and finished up on the outskirts of a village about two miles from the car.

You were absolutely worn out and as we sat down on a patch of grass along came a crowd of lady hikers who made a great fuss of you (I was totally ignored other than to supply your name) and then it was a succession of "Oh, isn't he lovely?" and "Can he have a biscuit?" etc., etc., and so I had to sit there and nod feebly at all this adulation you eagerly lapped up, concluding with actual lapping up of an ice cream cornet which one of the girls bought you. (I got nothing.)

As we wearily set off on the final homeward stretch, you kept looking at me and I could see those words ballooning out of the top of your head: "The next time we go on one of theses ridiculous jaunts, just make sure you know the way back. will you?"

As we trudged wearily along the lanes, another balloon appeared as you fixed me with a baleful look which reminded me of a typical Laurel and Hardy situation in which Hardy looks exasperatingly at Laurel and says, "Another fine mess you've got us into!" but the message in the balloon was "I've had enough of this. You go on, I'll follow later". With that, you just sat down and refused to budge despite all my pleas. So I had to sit down with you - for about 20 minutes. You know, if I'd had an upturned hat and a mouth organ we'd have made ourselves a fortune.

It seems very strange now strolling round the Burrows Lea woods without you and even stranger not to have that scratch at my office door almost regularly at 20 minutes to 11 every morning when one of the ladies would let you in and then you would come over to my desk and jump up with your front legs on my thigh for your regular morning massage. I had to stop whatever I was doing to give your back a good rubbing: then you'd be off again. Well, as I have said, you are being greatly missed but, of course, it is a great comfort for all of us to know that you are free from the burdens of age and are no doubt enjoying your new life in Spirit where we will all see you again in the fullness of time.

By the way, I would like you to do me a special favour, if you would. I want you to watch out for a West Highland Terrier, a white ball of fire who was in fact the brother you never knew, for we had him before you arrived. His name was Max. You will recognise him at once amongst all the other Westies, for his pure arrogance was his hall-mark which was apparent when he took over the entire household from the time we had him as a puppy. We were all nothing more than his personal valets, a situation compounded by the fact that we adored him, he knew it, and he played it for all that it was worth. When you see him, give him our love.

Enjoy your new life and, to borrow the words of a very famous lady film star whom you will probably never have heard of, but who had a saying: "Come up and see me some time", so we would say to you, dearly, beloved, Mick, "Come down and see us some time", especially when we go strolling in the woods where we have planted a nice flowering shrub to mark your final resting place.

Much love from us all

A Dog's Plea

1   Guide me with patience through my puppy days that I might quickly learn the ways you would have me follow.

2   Correct not my errors by using a stick to break my spirit for, between harsh blows, I will only turn and lick the hand that hits me, as I seek your forgiveness.

3   Treat me kindly, more kindly than others, perhaps, treat you, for no heart in this world will return that kindness more readily than this loving heart of mine.

4   Command me as you will, but speak with me often, and as a friend, for your voice can be the music of companionship, best conducted by the wagging of my tail.

5   Provide me with a warm home, indoors, when it is cold and wet and recognise that I am a home-loving creature; no more accustomed to living in the open air than you.

6   Keep my water bowl regularly refreshed and filled, that I may never suffer, simply by being unable to tell you when I thirst.

7   Feed me food that will keep me healthy enough to romp and play and grow, and stay at your side year by year. Share with me your time, then neither of us will feel lonely; let companionship be our joy; and allow me the privilege of sharing your comforts, and sitting at your feet.

9   Permit me to walk the pathway of life beside you, and I shall stand ready to protect you always, even with my own life, should you ever be in danger.

10 Dear friend, when, in the evening of my life I am old and ailing, losing my hearing, and failing in sight, be strong when I am weak, and prepare us both for our parting.

11 For our friendship's sake, do not prolong for me a painful end, by making vain effort to keep me from journeying on. Ensure only, that my life is taken gently. And then, know this. Despite any appearance to the contrary, I shall leave this world fully aware of your love, comforted by your kindness, thankful for your consideration, and having known that my life always, until its very end, was forever safe within your hands.

RR

Chapter 7

The Tests and Testimonies of Devotion

In sickness and in health and, seemingly, from beyond the jaws of death, the devotion of pet/person companions, each to the other, knows no bounds. From pet to person, from person to pet, does the two-way transmission of love come about only by pure accident? When lives are shared and problems are shared, could it not be by design?

Throughout their relationship, at some time either the pet or the person is likely to suffer illness and for those who, to over simplify it perhaps, prefer animals to people, there will be no end to which the person will go to try to bring relief to their pet companion.

During such illness, personal needs often take second place to ensure that funds are available for the payment of treatment or medicines for a pet. As far as that goes, however, the ability to provide additional help, through finance, is a decidedly a one way situation, person to pet, but it is also certain that not every person has the ability to provide finance. Where both pet and person are on equal, or near equal terms is, surely, in the sharing of love.

Costless, yet beyond price, are those mutual feelings of trust and devotion shared and exchanged during the pet/person relationship.

Appreciation shown, is appreciation understood, so it not surprising, to us at least, that so many of our friends provide testimony to their understanding of appreciation expressed by their companion, and demonstrated by that companion after they have crossed the Rainbow Bridge.

In Nottinghamshire, when a black stray cat gave birth to kittens in somebody's garden shed, the tiny arrivals certainly didn't have much of a start to life. That was until Miss JMS read the local paper.

"When we saw an appeal in the local newspaper for homes for the kittens, we phoned up and Arthur became part of the family soon afterwards. He was jet black, like his mother, an extremely loving cat despite his poor start, and used to love to be cuddled, even purring if he was cradled like a baby on his back. He wasn't entirely angelic though, he used to massacre the upstairs landing carpet until it was all pulled threads and bald spots. We tried many different scratching posts, but he still preferred that piece of carpet.

At the age of 18 months Arthur became gravely ill with Keys and Gaskell Syndrome. We nursed him carefully for over two weeks, but the pain became so intense that he couldn't bear us to touch him, never mind cuddle him. In the end he was put to sleep to end his terrible suffering. We were all very distressed by his death and I cried on and off for days afterwards.

Two days after his death I woke to a very familiar sound of cat claws being raked across the landing carpet. We had no other

cats at the time. I got up to have a look and the sound stopped. There was no one there.

Also, about the same time I was in the kitchen one-day and saw a movement out of the corner of my eye, a black shape was sitting in the kitchen doorway, just where Arthur used to sit. When I turned my head to take a closer look the shape was gone.

The strange happenings stopped after a week or so. I am convinced that Arthur came back to show us he still loved us despite being 'on the other side'. We have had several cats since and though two of them have since passed on, there have been no more incidents. The bond with Arthur was very strong and unique and if we have 100 cats, there will never be another one like him."

That unique bond is one that will be recognised and understood by many pet/partner people, and its outcome may be recognised by more than one person at the same a time, as M B from Australia was able to tell us.

"About 20 years ago we had a cat we called Little Cat. She suffered 2 bouts of Feline Enteritis which my partner and I nursed her through. Nursing her meant holding her and giving her lots of love along with the medicine she needed plus eye droppers of water. The poor thing got to the stage of just opening her mouth to take the medicine.

During one of these bouts I was playing music at our National Folk Festival which happened to be in my home State. I nursed *Little Cat between performances and when I was performing, Terry, my partner, nursed her. As a result of her sickness she had been difficult to toilet train, spending much of her kittenhood being ill. When she was well she wee-ed on the beanbag and I put her out. Next morning Terry found her dead. I felt awful.*

We had a low and large coffee table which we ate from whilst watching telly. One of her traits was to walk between our legs and the table, with her tail straight up with the end bent over. The end of her tail trailed across our food, on the table if we weren't careful. When she walked past us we automatically lifted our plates as she walked past.

A few days after she died we were having dinner. At the same time we both lifted our plates as we both saw her walk past. We were astounded. If only one of us had experienced it I would have thought it was fantasy. It was clear to us that our little cat had come back to visit those who loved her.

Most recently my partner Rob and I have had Baldrick, our most special cat die. Rob had a very special relationship with him and was distraught at his early death. Baldrick was Rob's first cat. Their early morning ritual was Baldrick sitting at the back door to come in and Rob letting him in to feed him and have his morning cuddle. A few days after he died Rob saw him at the back door and let him in. If it hadn't been for my experience with little Cat, Rob would have thought he had been fantasizing."

As a variety of events unfold in our lives, so they influence us. Unfold, of course, does not mean that the events have to include us, only that we have knowledge of them. When J W C moved into an old house in the Devon town of Newton Abbot, in England in 1967, her beloved British Blue, Tookey, was adamant that he was not going to remain in the sitting room after 9.30pm each evening. She recalls that his fur used to stand on end and that he always ran from the room. She also remembered often seeing a grey mist in the TV corner of this room! The family later learned that a suicide had been committed in the room. They also moved to another nearby town, Totnes, but this was only the beginning of J W C's story.

"In 1976 dear Tookey died and we moved soon after his death from Totnes to Southampton. One lunchtime I asked another teacher to swap dinner duties with me, as we had just adopted a new cat and I didn't want her to be alone all day. Arthur, the teacher, who also was a member of a Spiritualist Church, agreed adding "I'm glad because I noticed that little grey cat isn't beside you any more". Did my beloved Tookey move from Totnes to Southampton after all?

In 1987 after a long life my cat Muffers died, but by then she had encouraged a succession of strays to join our household, the last being Tim O'Flea (timid and riddled with fleas). Tim mourned Muffers and guarded her body as she lay in state awaiting burial and then often sat near her grave in the garden; however the following week we received a frantic phone call from our local vet asking us to take on Lucy.

Lucy had been the cook's cat at Avon Tyrell and after he moved up North, she was given in rapid succession to two other owners. So, rather disdainfully, she joined us in Southampton and spent many hours informing Tim that she had been used to a better standard of living but she was delightful and although very old she spent four years with us.

124

We returned to Devon in 1990 and life between Tim and Lucy became quite a battle for ownership of the central heating boiler. Lucy always won and hit Tim roundly off the top on every occasion. Unfortunately she died (aged above 14 we think) in 1992 and now Tim usually rests easily on the boiler but about every four or five weeks he recoils as if hit and jumps off the boiler - just as if Lucy has cuffed him yet again.

We often 'feel' our little black and white lady and see her out of the corner of our eyes. Perhaps to let her progress with her life, we should find another little lady cat?"

When R G N was 18 she was still living with her parents, and was going out with Martin who had a small black cat called Scamper-Jaques, whom he had "inherited" from a friend who had moved away. R G N spent most of her time over at Martin's house and the couple got to know Scamper-Jaques well, since he had a habit of waking them up in bed some mornings. With a few friends, she and Martin went out one evening but on their return, when R G N went to stroke Scamper as usual, instead of being his usual happy and purry self, he lashed out at her and growled.

"I called Martin in to see him and we discovered that his nose was dry, he wasn't well at all. A couple of days after, even after much medication and trips to the vets, Scamper-Jaques died (I think of a liver condition), everyone was very upset as he was so loveable.

A few days after that I was lying on the settee in the lounge watching TV, waiting for Martin to come back from work. As usual I heard Scamper-Jaques thundering down the stairs like a ton of bricks and watched as the cat flap "flapped" and rattled as he left the house. It was such a usual sound in the house that it didn't occur to me as being odd until I remembered he had died days earlier and that as the cat flap rattled I never actually saw him (or anything else) go through

it. I wondered if I'd imagined it, but when I spoke to Martin about it he said, "Oh, he's come back to see you too then?" Apparently both Martin and Majid (the lodger and friend) had experienced the same thing. I remember feeling very privileged and flattered that he should come back for me too, seeing as I was only a visitor to the house."

In a world where age makes a difference in many things, age obviously makes no difference when it comes to experiencing communication across the Rainbow Bridge. For many of our friends the experiences they have continue to be repeated through many years.

Their memories do not fade nor diminish, and neither does their wish to confidentially share those things that have come to mean a great deal to them. Many of our friends who contact us do not even mention their religious beliefs, some might indicate that they consider themselves to be 'Christians' without any further definitions, and yet others associate themselves with an understanding of the 'Spirit' with equal lack of further definition. To us, it matters not, since they all tell us of experiences that are often remarkably similar.

The uniting factor is that, without exception, their experiences are considered by them to be of value not only to themselves but to others also, when shared. Mrs B A S, who has a great deal of experience of the Spirit world, was quite clear about it when she said that she would like to share the comfort that both she and her husband have gained from the spirit realms on the passing of their beloved little dog Whisky, and indeed their beloved Alsatian bitch Tina also.

"They were both such lovely animals, and there was so much love from us to them, and them for us. I felt my heart would break when they passed. I am sure that others have felt this great pain also, this is why I would like to share my proof that they do survive and indeed come back to prove it.

Tina has made herself felt many times and both my husband and I have heard her bark in our bedroom during the night. There was no mistaking her.

My beloved Whisky is always around. He joins us at most sittings. I can smell his own peculiar smell. We hear him snore also. We know it's them without any doubt. I have a home circle that has been going for just over 20 years. We have had some wonderful evidence, but we keep our sittings out of the media.

People, even within the movement these days want flying trumpets etc, something fanciful, that they miss out on the wonderful happenings of true spirit contact."

The experiences of others have helped B A S and her husband throughout the years as they confirmed their own beliefs as understanding grew and they followed their own chosen path. Now, they hope that they in turn may help others heal that pain which is felt at the loss of the physical presence of beloved pet companions and, with the help of a strong bond of love, to guide those who are seeking knowledge towards finding a greater understanding of animal survival.

When Mrs K A C-C contacted us it was only coming up to the end of the first year since she had lost her grey and white cat, Paddington. Christmas had been but a couple weeks away when Paddington had died and, a year later almost, the memories remained and the terrible agony of missing her true friend was still there too, even though that friendship had hardly begun when Paddington died.

"I knew Paddington must be seriously ill as he stayed very tiny and hardly grew in the seven months we had him. My husband phoned me up whilst I was at work one afternoon from the pet shop where we always bought our supplies of cat food and where our previous cats had come from. He told me there was a gorgeous grey and white kitten there resembling a teddy bear, and did I want him to bring him home.

From my husband's description I was excited immediately at the thought of meeting him. Not being able to resist I said yes straight away. I loved this little kitten straight away and it was clear to everyone that came into contact with him that I favoured him slightly more than any of my other cats. He got a lot of attention from me and at night he'd come into our bedroom clamber on into the bed and sleep on my chest, sprawled out.

As the months went by I noticed that Paddington wasn't growing as he should be in comparison to the other five kittens in our flat that Tabitha our eldest cat had had. Knowing that something must be wrong I took him to our vets for blood tests. Although I should have been relieved that they came back OK, deep down I was sure that he wasn't going to live a long life and he was seriously ill.

On December 10th my husband got home from work and found Paddington collapsed, stone cold and barely alive. He'd been trying to hold on in hope that he'd see us when we got home. I was trying to comfort him as much as I could when my husband collected me from work. I talked to him all the way to the vets. I noticed he was trying to respond to my voice.

We had to have Paddington put to sleep, I was sobbing so much in the vets I wanted someone to reach out and make him all better, I'd never cried so much. I said goodbye to him and although I was told he was blind and couldn't see me I held his paw and noticed he was trying to wag his tail.

As he was put to sleep I looked around the room and wondered if he could see my face streaming with tears and my black eyes from my make up that had run. I cried all the way home and felt a tremendous loss. My husband was upset that he could do nothing to take my pain away, and kept apologising.

Wanting to hold on to Paddington's memory I went shopping to buy anything that resembled him and in a card shop found a small grey and white fluffy soft cat, that made a noise when you picked it up. It looked so much like him, it meowed and purred and meowed again. I took it home and sat it on my bookcase next to a couple of photos of Paddington.

A couple of days later when I was at home on my own I heard a noise coming from the living room. Thinking that one of my other cats had got up on the bookcase and knocked the cat I'd bought off it, I hurried into the living room. The cats were all asleep. There was nothing amiss.

The next time this happened was exactly a week after  Paddington had died and to the minute. This time I felt reassured that where ever he had gone in his after life he could have a sense of time and knowing what day it was in our life. This time I felt he was present in the room and I felt very cold with shivers going down my back. Part of me wanted to see him but I couldn't this made me feel sad.

On Christmas Eve my husband collected from our vets, Paddington in a little wooden sleeping cat. We'd decided to have him cremated. I couldn't wait to have him home, this helped me tremendously. We didn't have a garden as we lived in a three-bedroom flat and the vet suggested a wooden casket of some kind, the sleeping cat seemed appropriate.

One evening my husband took our dog out for a walk and I was feeling very low. I laid down on the carpet sobbing and reached out to embrace the sleeping cat I'd put under the Christmas Tree. As soon as I did this, the meows and purrs started from the fluffy cat. I was sure that Paddington was trying to tell me that he was alright, and very happy.

My husband wondered if getting another cat would be a good idea. There was no way another cat could ever take Paddington's place but, after a few weeks, we thought it could help ease the pain I was going through, and might help take my mind off it all. This time we went to a pedigree breeder.

We bought a lilac and cream Colourpoint Persian, and named him Magic for good luck. But our luck wasn't to be. Magic was ill when we had bought him and, with us not realizing at first, he started getting worse. We took Magic to the vets and he stayed overnight. My husband rang me from work the following day to say that the vets had been in touch with him and Magic had just passed away without any pain. This was about 12.20pm. Sure enough at 12.20pm again the following day the fluffy cat Meowed. Since that day I haven't heard anything more from the cat. I think Paddington has a play friend in his other world, and I now have two wooden sleeping cats as a constant reminder of my love for both of them."

J H B told us that when she lived in an early Victorian house Derbyshire she had two cats, Romny, and a real wild-cat named Venus and recalls one particular night, when the rain was pouring down and the winds were high. She was safe and secure in the house, but concerned about the storm, especially when she heard what sounded like a cat, crying, outside the door. Thinking it was either Romny or Venus she hurried to let them in and opened the door. A very appreciative cat ran in, and down the passage to the kitchen.

After battling with the elements to get the door closed again, J H B thought that she would feed her cats, made her way to the kitchen, and found that she now had three. Monty, as he was later named, had no intention whatsoever of going out into the storm again, he was home, and if not dry, soon would be.

"He made his home with us and attached himself to my husband, for no matter where Monty was as my husband came to the hall door, Monty was soon at the back door waiting to come in."

A post-office career move took the couple to Blackpool, with their cats, but little changed and Monty's attachment to J H B's husband continued. After a day working with the mail, and he was home settled for the night in an armchair, Monty always liked to be near him; but Monty was also a cat who, at other times, would not stay in.

"Well after a few years living here Monty died. I never knew how old he was - and we missed him a lot. I missed him coming in when my husband was at the front door. About three weeks later, or four, when the time came for my husband to come home, this black shadow used to come where the door used to be, but he had to come through a cupboard. He'd come across the living room floor and sit on the chair he as used to."

131

To avoid further confusion, we'll add a vital piece of information. The door to the kitchen in their Blackpool home had been changed from that which Monty knew. Structural alterations completed by J H B's son meant that where the door had once been, there was now a cupboard. However, Monty still followed the route he had known and, apparently ignoring the alterations, entered the kitchen by a now nonexistent doorway.

"He would only stay about ten minutes then out again the way he came in. This went on for a good six weeks, but my husband never saw him.

The last appearance of Monty was six years ago, when I had a very serious operation for cancer, of which I got cured. He began to come in again, but this time he came to me. This lasted quite a bit as I had to have another operation, and he stayed until I was better, but he came to me when I was on my own and I used to talk to him. I told him I am now getting better, so thank you for visiting me.

Only once more did I see him, and I think it was to say goodbye. This is the story of my ghost cat, Monty, who came back to us but only I could see him."

There had been an incident once when Monty had been 'lost' for some days and when he did eventually return home he said that he was 'in a very bad state'. J H B nursed him long into the night, comforting him and showing him that she cared for him, until he was better. Since his passing across the Rainbow Bridge, she says that she has often wondered whether this is why he came back to her, alone, when she was recovering from her operations. You will have noticed that only J H B could see Monty and for some people, when they alone have an experience it is difficult, at least, and sometimes downright impossible, to discuss what they have seen with others.

Sharing the knowledge of an experience, we believe, is beneficial, though the very thought of being ridiculed does not encourage us to tell even our closest friend some of the things we might be finding it difficult to believe ourselves. The closed mind is a barrier few would be willing to challenge, and we know from so many of the letters we receive that relate to events from the past, sometimes many years in the past, that an experience or encounter is never forgotten and that there is joy and relief when the opportunity to share them does eventually arise.

The friends who write to us, perhaps after reading an article or hearing one of our broadcasts, have obviously chosen the letter as their means of communication with someone who is, at first, a stranger. What then becomes apparent is that the writer wants to share their knowledge, and share their experiences, with others that will listen.

J J W, from the north of England, summoned up the courage to write to Evelyn to tell her about the experience she'd had some time earlier but, she freely admitted that she had never discussed it with anyone else, not even close family, and then added the comment that mattered.

"I've never told anyone, not even close family. I would like to, but I doubt that they would believe me."

A couple of years had elapsed before she put pen to paper to share her experience with us; a couple of years had elapsed since one of her two dogs had died.

"My family had had a succession of pets since I was a child - goldfish, dozens of rabbits, dogs and cats.

The "spooky" tale I have to tell is about one of our dogs, a lovely King Charles Spaniel girl named Cola. She was our first dog and was a much loved pet for many years. On the day that she died she suffered a number of heart attacks and was whisked away by the vet. That was the last time I saw her alive.

It was heartbreaking to receive the phone call that she had died. It seemed to me worse because I wasn't with her at the end to comfort her. I have nursed a couple of pets who have died but nothing out of the ordinary has happened afterwards. Anyway, that night I lay awake when suddenly I felt I must sit up. As I did so, a lovely breeze blew in front of me, it was warm, and had a familiar smell I couldn't recognise, but I slept after that.

The next day my Dad brought home Cola to be buried in our garden. I only then realised that the 'breeze' and Cola smelled the same. Since then it has comforted me to know that animals must have souls. Cola was simply reassuring me that she was still around!"

Reassurance can come in the simplest of ways and, for this young lady it came borne on a breeze, yet it took years before the comfort she was given could be shared.

When N L W wrote to us from Nottinghamshire it had been a couple of years for her also since the experience she wanted to share with others had taken place in her home. She had been waiting for a friend to call and decided to while away the time sitting in the lounge and doing a bit of cross-stitch. Collecting up her sewing she made her way to the lounge and on her way there she saw Sindy, her ginger cat, sleeping on the chair in the dining room. In the lounge she found her other two cats, Midge on one armchair and Sophie on the other.

"I sat down with Sophie. Then I heard the scratching post being used (this was out of my sight by the side of the settee). I just thought Sindy had come to join us, looked around waiting for her to appear from the settee and was amazed to see it was

a black cat and not a ginger Sindy at all. Midge and Sophie were still on the chairs. The black cat was my little Keppa who had died about a year before. I was so pleased to see her and she was happy - her tail told me that.

We had a special bond so maybe that's why she came to me. I must say I knew she was here because I had heard her mew and felt her jump on my bed. I've not seen or felt her since that day. I'm in my seventies and have had and lost many cats, but Keppa's the only one I have both heard and seen. Since she died I've got a little Japanese Chin dog and wonder if this frightened her away."

We can only wonder too, but doubt it somehow. Is it, perhaps, that contact for confirmation on those occasions was all that Keppa, or N L W, needed?

For some, like M B, who lives not far from the old Elstree film studios, the visible contact comes quite quickly. She wrote to tell us that only two weeks after her beloved cat, Jenny, passed over the Rainbow Bridge, at the age of 15 years, she had seen her again and felt her brushing against her legs. She had heard some old familiar sounds too, like Jenny lapping at her water dish. She had drank a lot in the last two weeks before she passed, M B, recalled. Needless to say, she was missing Jenny very much but still found time to share her experiences with us.

A letter we received in December 1997 clearly illustrated for us that the memory of an experience does not diminish. It had been over sixteen years previously that Miss M M M had an encounter that she wanted to share when she wrote to us from her home on the south coast of England

"At the time I had 3 cats, all ex-strays, but only one, Goldie, had come to me as a kitten. I was also patronised by a neighbour's cat, Blackie, who came fairly regularly for tea and

sympathy. All my cats had their own special eating place, Goldie's being on the kitchen bench.

In November 1981, then aged 10, she was killed by a dog. One day shortly afterwards Blackie arrived for his usual handout and jumped on to the bench where Goldie had been accustomed to take her meals. Suddenly his fur stood on end, he leapt down from the bench and literally inched his way on his stomach across the floor. Once he reached the open back door he took off at high speed. It was some days before he returned, but he never got on the bench again. I have to believe that Goldie was still in residence and had objected most strongly to Blackie's use of her eating place.

P.S. I was especially interested to read of other people who have felt a weight on their bed. I too have had this experience more than once (I have had a lot of cats) but until now have always put it down to my imagination."

Many people put things down to their imagination but we often hear from those whose new pet companions react to, literally, being put on the spot by a previous occupant of their newfound home. We too have similar experiences, of visiting cats shying away from a place where our own Puddy had made his own. The reaction is very clear indeed, as if the intruder had been aware of an unseen presence, had steered clear of it, or even had been visibly 'moved' by an unknown force.

There is no doubt about it, no visiting cat would ever have moved Puddy from his favourite spot when he was there, or even made an attempt, and particular 'places' do become very much associated with our special pets. From her home not far from Wast Water, in Cumberland, D M reminded us with her own experiences that 'places' can matter very much indeed.

"Some years ago I had two Siamese cats, a seal queen and a blue male (both neutered). Opposite our home was a bungalow with a low wall, and the blue-point, Nimrod, would wait on this wall every evening I was out, ready to greet me on my return.

Sadly he died quite young, and for some weeks afterwards, when I came home in the dark, there would be a pale shape on the wall where he used to sit. If I looked too hard, or approached, it would fade away, rather like a patch of mist, (although I knew that could not be the cause). I am convinced that this was Nimrod's spirit.

My seal point, Topaze, used to sit on the side-board in the evening and after I had gone to bed, would then jump down with a quiet thud and come to join me. For some time after she died, when lying quietly in bed, I would hear the same gently "thud" I used to hear when she jumped down. I could hear no other sound at all, not even traffic from the distant main road, or a night bird in the clump of trees at the back. At no time did I feel any fear at either the "apparition" or the noise, rather, that they were still with me in spirit. I have never had any experiences like these with any other deceased cat."

When we hear from some friends, sometimes it seems not to matter one iota whether it is a personal memory of a personal experience they wish to tell us of, or whether it is their knowledge, and belief, in the experience of someone they know and trust. What does seem to matter most is that the experience is shared, even after many years.

Dr L P C in South Wales had known for years that her mother had seen her British Blue cat, Kaliph, after his death, many years before she shared the news with us.

"Unfortunately I do not have a date for the sighting but I will give you the details I have.

We had Kaliph in the late 1970s, he was a British Blue shorthair, the first pedigree cat we owned. My mother was extremely attached to Kaliph, she felt very sorry for him as he had been incorrectly neutered. He still had one hidden testicle and this affected his temperament making him frustrated.

We were very sad when at only $6\frac{1}{2}$ years old he had to be put down due to feline leukaemia. This would have been around 1984-5. We were lost without him and soon acquired another British Blue, Max, in 1985. Max was perfectly healthy until he caught a virus at about 6 months. This left him rather thin and he never truly recovered from it, eventually having to be put down in April 1993 at the age of 8.

My mother was going upstairs one evening, we think it was in 1992, when she saw a grey shape on the landing at the exact spot where Kaliph used to sit. As she went to pass, it vanished. A few months later she was going upstairs with Max, when he suddenly stopped by the landing hissing and obviously frightened. He was looking towards the spot where Kaliph had been sighted and refused to pass it.

I now think that Max could see Kaliph and that the latter had come to 'collect' Max - who was already quite frail. It would indeed have startled Max to see Kaliph who was virtually his double! I enclose pictures of both cats from which you can see they are indeed very alike. I am sure myself that our pets do live on and may occasionally visit their favourite haunts.

J R L's experience in London, where she lived and worked, left her in no doubt whatsoever after her beloved pet companion Peter died in February 1995 aged 16. Even though she knew the end was near for her friend, after nursing him through his illness for several months she was devastated at his passing and, years afterwards can still burst into tears when she thinks of him.

"I had two cats but Peter was always with me, slept with me, got up with me, knew when I went to work walked to the door to say goodbye and was always waiting at the door on my return. I woke at 4am the morning after his death and I saw my beloved boy sitting at the foot of "our" bed framed in gold.

At the time I worked in an office and each day took the mail to the post office and each time I was aware of Peter accompanying me, sitting on my shoulders as he used to do. I could feel his soft fur and lovely bushy tail around my face. I sometimes feel him on my shoulders now.

About 6 months after he died, one evening I went into the hall and saw Peter half way up the stairs. I said "hello babe" as I always did, walked passed and realised Peter was no longer in this life. I do believe we shall see our pets again, and I quote from the Bible - Revelations - Behold I make all things new."

Even among those people who stoutly deny that there cannot be any 'after-life' whatsoever, there are a great many who will unequivocally comment that, "cats have nine lives."

Four Feet In Heaven

Your favourite chair is vacant now
  No eager purrs to greet me
    No softly padded paws to run
      Ecstatically to meet me
        No coaxing rubs, no plaintive cry
          Will say it's time for feeding
            I've put away your bowl
              And all the things you won't be needing.

But I will miss you, little friend
For I could never measure
The happiness you brought to me
The comfort and the pleasure.
And since God put you here to share
In earthly joys and sorrow
I'm sure there'll be a place for you
In Heavens' bright tomorrow.

Anon.

Chapter 8

May Angels Fly Thee Home

Friends who talk to us about their pet/person relationships include some that hold pretty strong views about those relationships after many years experience, those who are just discovering that there really is such a meaningful relationship, and those whom, even with experience, still find that if they keep an open mind they have both a lot to learn, and a great deal to share. Firmly placing ourselves in the latter group, well, if not firmly, at least with some hope of getting there, we at least have the benefit of not only hearing questions, but also hearing what some suggest might be answers.

Can a friend ever be replaced? For many who suffer the final breakdown in a long established and strong pet/person relationship there is little doubt that their answer would be, no. However, for someone in the same situation who has a strong belief that the word 'final' could not apply, would certainly suffer because of a parting, yet might also point out that friendships often introduce us to more friends.

What are friends for anyway? During our lifetime friends come and go, a few we keep from our earliest days, others we only find late in life; all are valued but, if we are fortunate, few are forgotten. Volumes could be written to answer the last question, and learned people could make a career out of researching the answer that each of us would give, based upon our individual experiences, actions, and hopes.

The bonds established between people in their friendships, is not only mirrored in the pet/person relationships but seem often to be raised to new heights, increased in strength, and founded on a loyalty that is exceptional. That loyalty, we believe, can be seen being demonstrated in all kinds of ways

There is a family now living near Boston, in the USA, that left the UK not too long ago. A major career step forward was the incentive for D J L's husband to lead his family into a new life but it also meant that D J L would have to step back, temporarily at least, from pursuing her own career as a Midwife, and their three children would need to adapt to a new way of life.

As might be expected, the future seemed uncertain and even daunting from a distance. While opportunity was definitely knocking, friends and family nearby would become distant friends and family. Pet/person relationships had also been a feature of family life but past friends and present pets were all to be left behind. The family left England to take up temporary residence in a superior accommodation while they decided exactly where to settle; and the homesickness began. This was not unexpected and, to be fair, did not affect them all equally. Early in 1999 D J L wrote to tell us of her recent experience, and its outcome.

"On Tuesday evening I was sitting in the rocking chair reading and a cat started purring behind me, I listened, sure it was Theo our old black and white cat. After 30 seconds or so I turned round to look at it, but of course there wasn't one there and the purring stopped. Anyway, yesterday I decided to go to the Animal Shelter (there are several around but I only found one listed in the phone book) to see if there was a cat there waiting for us.

Well, I walked around some of the cages and the cats inside either ignored me or just looked back until I got to one cage

and a little grey tabby came straight up to the bars to be petted. Her name was Cleo, she had been there just 4 days. She was like a mixture of all the cats we've ever had. She purred as low as Theo, she was petite with a small head and biggish ears (like Oscar and Alice), her coat was short haired but really thick (like Jasper), her colouring and markings were like Hamilton, George and Alice (again), her paws were all grey (like Drifter, one of Oscar's kittens who went to live with Julie) and she was really friendly and affectionate. Needless to say I didn't look any further.

I went back to the lady in the office and asked if I could adopt Cleo, only to be told that she was very shy and timid, wouldn't go to anyone to be petted and they weren't sure how she would be with kids. Anyway, I talked them into letting her come home with me. As we were leaving they said that as soon as I let her out of the box at home she would probably run off and hide for a while, so keep her in one room to begin with. They said she would need to get to know us before we could pet her (she hadn't liked being petted in the shelter), and to watch her with the kids. Off we went. We got home just as T... got in from

school (he was so happy he cried, we hugged and I cried too!). We opened the box and Cleo looked at us.

She jumped out of the box, spent the next three hours exploring the whole apartment, meowing and purring as she went and coming to us every couple of minutes to be stroked and rubbed. When the girls got home from school (more crying and hugging), she introduced herself to them and carried on exploring. Same again when M.... got home!

She likes to be with us all the time; she follows me around and slept on the floor at the end of our bed. She jumped up onto M....'s pillow at one point during the night. She's been sitting on my lap most of the morning, purring and being stroked. At the moment she's curled up on the chair next to me. We couldn't have found a more typically 'L...... Family' cat if we'd spent a year looking. She seems really content, she's certainly not shy or timid with us, loves attention and gets on fine with the kids.

We've all been feeling pretty homesick lately, I think Cleo will help make everyone feel better. We all missed having a cat, but as you know, you can't make do with any old cat. I like to think that Theo came and purred behind me to let me know that it was time for me to go and find Cleo. A psychiatrist would have a field day with me!"

Perhaps many a psychiatrist might, but not one that had even the slightest inkling about pet/person relationships. As was confirmed by the number of cat names D J L mentioned, the past 'pet/people' relationships in this case had been very important to everyone in the family.

Since the family was in temporary accommodation, albeit of a high standard, they were by no means settled, and a new pet had not been among their priorities. Later correspondence showed us that just the presence of Cleo has did indeed make a difference to the family so, was D J L right in even thinking that Theo still had the interests of his old friends at heart, from across a greater distance than just the Atlantic Ocean?

Only a hundred miles or so away from where the Atlantic rollers hit the shores of England, J B E and his wife had, some years earlier, lost their schipperke bitch "The Whizz Kid" at 18 years of age. They were both heartbroken, wanted another furry friend, but it had to be an older dog. They went to their local animal shelter, Little Valley, where they were interviewed and questioned, and then asked what sort of dog they wanted. After confirming that they were seeking a small terrier-type bitch, about five years old, the couple were given a list of animal and kennel numbers, and, as J B E says,

"At the first kennel number I saw a scruffy little girl with the loveliest eyes in the world, and she looked at me and said "Please?" and I lost my heart and fell in love at first sight. In no time at all our home was inspected, forms were signed, and we were taken over by our new "boss."

She was called Tacker, but as we had, years ago, a lovely beagle called Tosca, we altered her name slightly. I have had dogs all my life, but never have I had a dog so obedient, so affect-ionate or devoted.

Soon after having her, my wife had to go into a resid-ential home, and Tosca took over as the lady of the house. As I live in the country she had some excellent walks - but

for a lady she is a terrible 'sniffer'.

She goes everywhere with me, demanding a ride in the car (front seat of course) every day, and spends the rest of the day lying on her 'couch'. For some reason she wants to go up to bed every evening (she has a bed at the foot of mine) soon after 7pm, but if there are any visitors she stays up, like a perfect hostess and helps entertain her guests.

About 6.30 every morning she jumps on the bed, sits on my chest, gives me a lick and says, "Morning, boss, are you O K?" When I say "Yes", she settles down until breakfast time. She makes a lonely life full of happiness just by being there and sharing her life with me. I owe a huge debt of gratitude to Little Valley for bringing us together, I think we are a real team - maybe not First Division, but who cares?"

The extent to which a pet/person relationship can provide friendship in times of need are certainly understood and appreciated by F B E and a helping paw was also waiting not only for P S when she needed it, but also for another 'friend' as well. Her experiences began after a collie-cross called Willow, belonging to her daughter, came to stay with her after her old dog, Titus, died.

"We were out walking on a footpath when I climbed a stile, caught my foot in some brambles, and down I went, sitting for a while, stunned, and bleeding from the nose. Willow came and sat beside me, offering much comfort. There were two more stiles to negotiate before we got home, and each time she came and stood by to make sure I got over safely. Another time, when she was at home with my daughter, they had gone to see the horses and the little sheltie dog, Toddy, had been accidentally kicked. He was shocked, but otherwise unhurt, and my daughter laid him on her jersey in a loose box while she finished seeing the horses.

146

When she went to get him she found that Willow had fetched a
stick and laid it beside him to show her sympathy. She loves to
play with sticks, and obviously felt that it would cheer Toddy
up."

Can a friend ever be replaced? The question is often asked, and many would give a negative answer but, surely, it was more than just fortunate that J B E found a new friend in 'Tosca' when he needed the comfort of companionship. Similarly, the consideration shown by newcomer 'Willow' to both PS and to a little sheltie had value for each of them. Other visitors to the Little Valley Animal Sanctuary, where JBE, had found his friend Tosca, were equally delighted to find a new friend there, 'Dinnyham' and, after eight months JMH provided a progress report on their good fortune and lucky find.

"The time has gone very quickly and 'Dinnyham' has changed quite a lot. Every day he gains in confidence. When we collected him from Little Valley he was very reluctant to get into the car, but now you only have to mention the word and he is ready to go. We had bought him a few presents, which he soon opened when we got home. He was so excited he wanted to pick them all up together!

At first, he was getting quite stiff after a walk, which gave us a bit of concern. We started giving him a supplement and cod liver oil and even tried some spiritual healing with an animal healer. Now he very rarely gets stiff at all. He runs, swims and plays and seems very happy. It gives us a lot of pleasure to see him bouncing around and enjoying himself. Due to his lovely nature he has made lots of friends. He loves cuddles and being stroked. He throws himself heart and soul into playing and has a ferocious growl when he gets excited. We quickly realised it was his way of talking to us!

When our last dog died we didn't think it would be possible to get close to another so quickly, but 'Dinnyham' is special. He is brilliant."

AEE visited Little Valley to help photograph the animals there for a special RSPCA window at its Crediton shop. She didn't anticipate the result of coming face to face with a poor, badly neglected, little cat who was being cared for there on what was to be a fateful, and fortunate, day.

"Immediately I saw Floss my heart went out to her. She was skin and bone, and had lost much of her fur, as her previous owner had not treated her for fleas, this had formed an allergy, badly affecting her coat. Floss was a little cat that many would look at, feel sorry for, but walk on. I could not do that.

When the door of her pen was opened Floss immediately rolled over so I could tickle her tummy. It seemed that despite being badly let down by humans she clung to the hope that here, perhaps, was someone who would restore her faith in human nature. I couldn't forget her, and took my husband to see her. She was ours within a week. When our vet saw her he was amazed at her condition, but was confident that I would soon put her to rights.

Floss settled in straight away and didn't take long to settle into the animal's mealtime routine. She was soon exploring the garden, climbing trees and pond-watching. Could anyone PLEASE tell me how I can stop her catching frogs?

After three months with us Floss is now completely transformed from the pathetic little cat I first saw. She has gained weight, now has a furry tail instead of a bottle brush, and has grown most of her fur, which is turning into a lovely silky coat. She is most affectionate and loves her tummy tickled whilst rolling on the garden path, a bed, or chair. Floss gets on well with Jack, our rescued collie, and they sleep on the settee together, whilst she and Kitty, our seventeen year old cat, merely tolerate each other.

We feel we are nearly there, and get there we will! How anyone could allow a little cat (or any animal) to deteriorate so before taking any action never ceases to amaze me. I wonder what

they would think of her now? I shall never regret seeing Floss that April day and being the one privileged to restore her back to health and help her to regain her faith in human nature. We look at her sometimes and feel sure that she can't believe her luck.

Here's to a long, happy and healthy life with us, Floss!"

It seems to us to be far from co-incidental that so many people can find so many pets with little or no effort, when one or the other, the pet or the person, seems most in need of a friend. When the person is least expecting it, up pops a pet that not only needs a home and companionship, but is also a pet that fits the bill as far as the person is concerned, the home they possess is concerned and, in some cases, fit the bill for the other occupants of that home, be they other pets or just more people. Can we really ignore 'selection' and who chooses whom?

D A, from her home in the South West of England had something to say which again made us look at the question.

"Sable was old; the notice on his kennel said so. There was no denying the grizzled white muzzle, the spread paws or the slackness of skin around his puzzled eyes. He was a German Shepherd, and most of his life had been lived in pleasant ways until his owner died and he was taken over by a less sympathetic human, and finally abandoned. He reached the kennels via the Inspectorate and the long arm of the law, and his dismal cries of protest could be heard day and night.

I had lost my beloved German Shepherd, Sherpa, the year before and sorely missed him; I had to wait some months before the due processes of law were complete and I could adopt Sable and take him to his new home.

Of course, he was puzzled by his new surroundings but like all dogs, he accepted it, for what else can a dog do? They are powerless in the hands of the humans who own them, and have to accept the good, and the bad - but if it is good, how they respond!

My dogs have always had a basket by my bed and this was a very new idea to Sable. At first he was very reluctant to mount stairs, but quickly became used to the idea and obviously liked it - he was usually first to go to bed at night. He quickly showed me he loved to roam in the garden and walk in the forest on Haldon but he hated men! He chased our gardener down the drive one evening and objected so strongly to our milkman taking the empties that he rushed out and bit him! Fortunately the milkman is a friend, and only said 'he is protecting you'. And so he was, and became devoted to us.

Although his back legs were failing, he tried hard to gambol and play with our other dogs and could always be found lying patiently by us when we were weeding or digging.

Sadly, the day inevitably dawned when he tried to get out of bed in the morning and his back legs would no longer obey his wishes. He lies asleep beside Sherpa under the grass by the kitchen window; and they probably compare notes as they run in the Elysian Fields. We had nine happy months together and the moral of my story is 'When you are looking for a pet, please don't ignore the old dog or cat'. You will not have them for long, but they will bring you just as much happiness."

D A was quite right; age matters not a jot when companionship counts and whether living together in a pet/person relationship for a short while or a long period of time it is the togetherness that all of our friends remember.

From the USA we heard about Rudy from D L M, about her experiences after Rudy died, and about how valuable the eight years she had previously enjoyed with her beloved cat were to her; and, we suggest, to them both.

"My husband and I were living with his parents while we were constructing our new home. However, Rudy died before we moved in. This cat was like a child to me, we often felt as though he was human instead of feline. He had such a wonderful personality and so many facial expressions. I'm sure he probably thought we were cats! I do believe that he chose to live with me. I knew this only a few months after he was given to me.

After moving to a new apartment, I found out that I could not keep him in the apartment, so I sent him to live with a friend. It was only a few weeks later and I couldn't bear it any longer. My friend told me that he literally mourned while he stayed with him, too!

So, I decided to move to another apartment just so he could be with me. He wouldn't leave my sight for days! My experience after his death was the actual night he died. He contracted

Feline Immune Deficiency Disease from a stray cat at my mother-in-law's house and I nursed him for the last year of his life. He died in my arms looking directly into my eyes.

Later that night, my husband and I decided to take him to our new home that wasn't quite finished. It was very strange, but I had a sense that I needed to take him there just to see where we would have lived. Moving would not be the same without Rudy in our lives. We built a fire in the fireplace and just sat there remembering every cute thing this cat had ever done (and crying!). I felt as if he were right there with us the entire time. We took him room to room. It wasn't until we were leaving that the strangest thing happened.

When I opened the front door to leave, I heard him meow. My husband acted as if I had lost my mind. It was Rudy's meow, because I heard it not only with my ear, but also with my heart. It was as though Rudy were telling me that it would be O. K. to live here, that he would be here with me.

On that night, my husband's mother had been with us. She didn't hear a cat meow and my husband denied hearing anything. He said it was probably the November winds. But, a few nights later as we lay in bed he asked, "Why do you suppose Rudy meowed for us the other night?"

At that moment I knew it wasn't only me who had heard his little voice. He does live on ... and before that day, I would have thought a story like this was totally crazy.

Thank you for allowing me to share this message with you. God Bless!"

We appreciated the blessing, and knew we had to share the message, just as we had to share the messages we received from another of our American friends, N E M. Previously, we've included her experiences with Misty Baby Cat,

Shadesie, Sage and others and are very much aware that she has had lots of psychic experiences with her cats.

"Yes, that is true. Actually all the members of my family are psychic. Many of us have displayed various types of psychic abilities for many generations. In fact, my Great Aunt Lucy was said to have been a witch. I just think she was a very modern woman, way ahead of her time, who was possibly feared and certainly disliked by other family members. They were very jealous of her.

We grew up in an atmosphere where our psychic abilities were an everyday thing, and not at all unusual. I had my first (remembered) psychic encounter when I was 10 or 11. It was with my dear Uncle, who had moved to Indio, about 350 miles from us. I really missed him. One night I dreamed about him being in a bowling alley. I could hear the pins being knocked down and everything. I did not know at the time that he was really into bowling. However, back to cats.

I had my first psychic encounter with my beloved cat Ariadne, when she was only a few hours old. She was born in 1970 in my sister's apartment in Isla Vista, during the burning of the Bank of America. I had waited all day for the birth and finally gone back to my own apartment. No sooner than I got there, the phone rang. Esmeralda had at last had her babies. I went right back over.

Since Essy was my cat, I had first choice of the 6 kittens. I took one look at all those little black and white darlings, and immediately picked out the one who became my Ariadne Precious. She knew she was mine and she reached out her paw to me.

After I moved back home for the summer, when she was about 3 months old, she was gone for 3 days. I dreamed about her coming back to me. I saw her coming through the back picket fence. The next day she came back just exactly like I had

dreamed. It was then that I knew she was very, very special..
She was my dearest friend and companion for 17 1/2 years. She
crossed the Rainbow Bridge on Dec 3rd 1987, and I still miss
her.

Another experience involves my beautiful and beloved Emrys
Valentino, my little Kitten of Light. He was my only orange
kitty, and I loved him dearly. I had gone to get the May kitties
their birthday presents the Friday before Mother's Day, and he
was at the store. Well, it was truly love at first sight but I didn't
take him that day. I already had cats, and I didn't need
another one; but he was free with a $25 purchase.

Well, Monday couldn't come soon enough. I went straight back
to that store and brought that little sweetheart home. He really
did pick me. My sister said, iI knew you would go back for
himî. It was love at first sight. I lost him in October of 1996 to
a rare liver disease. It struck on Sunday and by Wednesday he
was gone. It was just so fast and unexpected. He wasn't ready
to die, and I wasn't ready to lose him. Often I see him sitting
around the house, and he is so real I call out to him.

One last thing. I have lived in my house since I was in high
school. It will be 33 years in June. In this home we have had
countless cats, and most of them are buried in the yard. We,
that is my family and I often see them, or their spirit floating
around. I think one reason we see them more often than some
people is because we are still in the same place. I don't know if
I would see them so often if I moved to a strange place."

If N E M ever does consider moving she may revise her
conclusion that she and her past friends communicate,
visually, because they are in the same place after thirty three
years when she learns of the three thousand mile move made
by D J M, and how Theo still found her.

We've already pointed out what most accept, that friendships
lead to more friendships and through our friend J M W in

Grand Cayman, we learned that J W in the USA had experienced something that, while she never thought of it as a paranormal experience, convinced her that her cat, Murphy, had quite specifically 'chosen' her. How (good) news does travel.

"We were grocery shopping a couple of years ago, and it was after dark when we returned to the van. There was only one other car, parked next to us. This little white cat with marmalade tabby markings came up and meowed.

I had raised Persians for 10 years, and had household cats as well. I didn't need another cat. But he stayed around, so I told my husband that if he crawled in the van on his own, we would take him home. I no sooner said it, than in he went.

My husband continued putting groceries in, and the cat didn't come out. So we brought him home. After calling around to the vets, advertising in the paper and calling a dealer I knew in that particular shopping mall, we had him neutered,

He turned out to be the best all around cat we had ever had. He reminded me so much of three marmalade tabby cats that were favourites of mine, and had died, Morris, Taffy and Muffin. So I named him Murphy after them.

In January 1998 I had respiratory failure, and was rushed to ER, put on a ventilator, and was in ICU for almost 2 weeks. While I was gone, my husband and daughter disposed of 2 dogs and 1 cat. Then my husband told me that the girls who were cleaning my house fell in love with Murphy. I told him they couldn't have him, and made it plain that he was MY kitty! When I came home, Murphy started following me everywhere I went. When and wherever I sit, he's there, loving all over me.

When I tell him the story of the 2 girls and what I told "Papa",
he goes ecstatic, just like he knows what I'm saying. We love
him dearly. I wouldn't trade him for any registered cat."

M Ḃ is a person who has no doubts whatsoever about the
selection process and was good enough to make her views
known to us together with a report on her experiences of cats
choosing her.

"I believe that all our cats chose us. Let me tell you a bit about
them. Isis is an almost 3 year old black female. We rescued her
from the SPCA when she was about 6 weeks old. I went there
to look at the kittens and every one of them totally ignored me.
Except for Isis.

I picked her up first, played and put her back in the cage so
that I could look at the other cats. The entire time, Isis stood on
her back legs, with her front legs thrust thru the bars of the
cage, meowing loudly. Once I had seen all the cats, I decided
that if she wanted to go home with me that much, she could.

Osiris showed up on our doorstep this past Halloween. At the
time he was still a kitten. All black with big gold eyes. Like
Isis, he had a small sprinkling of white hairs on his chest. My
boyfriend told me he was very friendly, but I had my doubts.

One morning I was leaving for work and this kitten plopped
down at my feet, rolled onto his back, and asked me to scratch
his tummy. I started feeding him and he was always happy to
get the food, but was more interested in being loved on. Finally
we decided that being an all black stray at Halloween could be
dangerous for him, so we took him in.

By far, the most interesting story is that of our middle fur
baby, Bastet. In the summer of 1998 we had only Isis, who had
just turned a year old. I started having this recurring dream
where Isis slowly faded from a sleek black cat with green eyes,

158

to a beautiful white cat with blue eyes, then she went back to her original self.

This carried on for a bit and then the dreams changed. One half of Isis, from the nose back to the tip of her tail, went white, with the eye on that side being blue. Then she split, as an amoeba does, into two cats. I knew the white cat was named Bastet.

At some point my boyfriend (we live together) started having the dreams as well. When we would compare what happened in the dreams, the details matched. We described the white cat, and our descriptions were the same. We checked all the local shelters, but no white cats.

One beautiful Saturday, we met my sister and nephew at a big flea Market. As we walked thru the gate, I was hit by a sudden flash of knowledge, Bastet was here. The first two pet shops I checked had no kittens at all. As we were walking out of a fish shop, I saw a store across the way and knew that was where she was waiting. I entered the store, and made my way to the back. All I found was a little tabby.

Beginning to wonder if my instincts were off, I turned to leave. Standing between me and the door was a little girl cuddling a small bundle of white fur. I asked her if that was her new kitty, and she replied "No, I was just playing with her. Here, you hold her," and thrust the kitten at me. I took her, and she purred happily and gave me little kitty kisses. Then she crawled up my arm, settled on my shoulder, and fell asleep. Just as Isis was prone to do at that age. After having my boyfriend meet her, we knew it was our dream cat. We paid the adoption fee and took her home. The store had told us that she was 10 weeks old, but our vet felt it was more like 6. It had been 6 weeks before that the dreams started. I feel that when she was born, she started calling to us to come save her.

At the time we adopted her, she was badly malnourished and had a severe protozoan infection. With the help of our wonderful vet we nursed her back to health. She is now a much-loved part or our family, as are Isis and Osiris."

Our friend M was not sure whether her experiences would be termed supernatural, or not, but she was very much aware that a very strange bond had existed between herself and her cat, Estralia, throughout the $2^{1}/_{2}$ years they had been together. M did have another cat as well but, as she put it;

"Estralia and I were fast friends. What do I mean? Well, when I brought her home, I just felt like I had known her forever, like it was destiny for her to be with me. I had a cat named Herman when I was younger and the death of him just made me so sad. I did not have another cat for years and years.

Estralia looks a lot like Herman but acts different. She also does strange things; I know most cats do strange things but this is beyond the normal strangeness. Example: She will not leave my side when I am home. She follows me from room to room. She sleeps on my feet when I am sitting down, when I am lying down she sleeps on my chest. She is very protective of me.

My sister came to live with me some years ago and she hated her. When my sister came around, she made her go away. She also, at times, runs through the house meowing at a very high pitch; I always know what she wants by her cry. It is like I can read her mind. She knows my soul and I hers. We are very close and I know it sounds very weird. However, it is really true. Estralia is a Spanish name, and in English it means star she is my star. I love her very much and just feel very close to her. My other cat and I don't share the same bond with her. Sometimes I believe Estralia is reincarnated maybe she is someone who has left this world that I loved, and she is watching over me. Who knows?"

D L extended the subject of 'returning from the beyond' when he shared the experiences he and his father had a few years ago,

"My father had a cat named Lightning that was solid black, except for a tiny patch of white on his underbelly. The cat was stone deaf from birth, and his "meow" was a barely audible squeak, almost like a mouse in pain. As a "Godgifted" compensation (so we believed) for his handicap, the cat was gifted with extraordinary speed, hence his name. You had to see it to believe it. He was not big, but he was a world champion "mouser," among other things. Lightning killed not only mice and rats, but snakes (my father lives on a farm) squirrels, and he once killed a full-grown possum!

He loved to be petted, but hated being picked up and held. My father came home from work one day and found Lightning lying dead in the road, run over by a car. He was about 5 years old. My dad was heartbroken.

Several months later, a STRAY cat wandered up into the yard, while my dad was working in his shop. The cat was solid black, with a small white patch on his underbelly, was stone deaf, and had a barely audible "meow," like a mouse squeak! Dad named him Lightning Jr.

He loved being petted, but hated being picked up and held. In the short time he was there, he was a "world champion mouser" also. Speed and all. He was hit and killed in the road 5 months later, about 40 feet from the spot where the beloved "first" Lightning had lost his life. That's the last we ever saw of him."

So, who among us can say that lightning never, ever, strikes twice in the same place? The likeness between the two cats was not just a case of colouring, their mouse-catching capabilities made an impression on D L and his Dad who welcomed two cats into their home, without doubt, but still wonder whether they had encountered just one.

The cat that G K encountered did not have a double and she was left in no doubt about which out of the two of them of them, pet or person, had conducted the selection procedure.

"I went to the Humane Society because my sister volunteers there and I was looking for another cat. She said she had the perfect one there for me. I was introduced to the one she had in mind. Then I saw Kelly Jo. She came running in and jumped on my lap.

They said she did a lot of biting and scratching and had an "attitude" and would probably never find a home. I'm convinced she wanted me as much as I wanted her. So I of course I adopted her. They said I would probably have to get her de-clawed. I said never! To this day, Kelly Jo and me are very close. She does scratch me on occasion, once she got my eyeball; I'm never mad, upset etc. To me Kelly Jo is loveable, to just about anyone else she is a "devil kitty". She knew I was the right one for her, and she was right.

Whatever the attitude, or personality, of a pet is, when the companion contract is confirmed twixt pet there are no questions asked. Jerome K Jerome once pointed out that a dog;

"never makes it his business to inquire whether you are in the right or in the wrong, never bothers as to whether you are going up or down upon life's ladder, never asks whether you are rich or poor, silly or wise, sinner or saint. Come luck or misfortune, good repute or bad, honour or shame, he is going to stick to you, to comfort you, guard you, and give his life for you....."

A Man's Best Friend

A faithful dog will play with you,
And laugh with you, and cry.
He'll gladly starve and stay with you,
Nor ever reason why.
And when you're feeling 'out of sorts'
Somehow he'll understand.
He'll watch you with his shining eyes
And try to lick your hand.

His blind, implicit faith in you,
Is matched by his great love,
The kind that all of us should have,
In the Master up above.
When everything is said and done,
I guess this isn't odd,
For when you spell 'DOG' backwards
You will see that you've found GOD.

Chapter 9

The Literature of Love;
Poems and Pieces

"Until he extends the circle of his compassion to all living creatures, man will not himself find peace."

Albert Schweizer

Down through the centuries people have expressed their thoughts about their pets by putting pen to paper or, more recently, fingers to keyboards, or voices on to tape. There have been professional playwrights, academics, historians, diarists, poets, and everyday people and, without exception, they all had, and have, something to share with us. We consider them, writers past and present, as friends one and all whose work should be shared with others;

TAB
Tab is loving, warm and sleepy,
Tab is mean and cruel and creepy,
He's a menace, then delightful,
Pert and playful, cross and spiteful;
Tab will steal food that he hates
Then sneer at tid-bits on a plate.
He spits, and claws his playmate's fur
Then cuddles up to him, to purr,
Ignores me with complete disdain
Then coyly rolls, inviting a game;
I try to coax him on my lap,
He's off, tail up and through the flap.
For sitting on, laps have to be

Supporting knitting, or hot tea,
At night I like him safe at home,
But that's when he decides to roam;
I call in vain, then go to bed
Imagine him run over - Dead?
Get up again. Of course, he's there,
Fast asleep in the best armchair.

Collections of dried flowers and grasses,
Tastefully arranged in vases,
Are there to sniff, and pat, and paw,
Or possibly knock to the floor;
Then innocent half-closed eyes smile back,
"As if I'd do a thing like that."
Going out is quite a feat,
He trots beside me down the street.
I pick him up and march him home,
Retrace my steps - the bus has gone.
He claws the carpets, tears the nets,
Costs a fortune at the Vet's,
He drives me mad with sheer frustration
But how dull my day would be
Without my Tab, my pet relation

Lynn Scally.

In the opinion of Erma Bombeck, "Every puppy should have a boy" a comment to which we would only add one word, "Every puppy should have a caring boy."

Many of those who work with organisations that care for animals, discarded and previously uncared for, will recognise the reminder, timely at any time of the year, that our friend Elizabeth Hampton provides in her poem;

The Christmas Puppy

The rescued pup looks desolate,
How can she realise
Her future was uncertain
As a Yuletide gift surprise?
The kids had many other toys
She soon became a bore,
That tiresome Christmas puppy
Who puddled on the floor.

Margaret Kernoghan might well have been the one who comforted that Christmas puppy since her words add an appropriate reminder;

Oh, the saddest of sights
In a world of sin
Is a little lost pup
With his tail tucked in !

And in "Dog's Eyes" the progress of the pup that might not have been appreciated past the feast of Stephen, is graphically drawn by J R E;

"Far more than his bark, a dog communicates through his eyes - from a soulful half-raised eyebrow when denied a special treat to the wide and sparkling 'Yippee ! We're going for a walk!'. Perhaps nothing can wrench the heart of a dog lover more than the pitiful, hardly-daring-to be-hopeful gaze of an abandoned dog waiting to be adopted."

"The average dog has one request to all humankind. 'Love me.' "
Helen Exley

"To a man the greatest blessing is individual liberty- to a dog it is the last word in despair."
Wm. Lyon Phelps.

In the first quarter of the 19th century William Hone was compiling books, including letters from friends, who have become veritable mines of information and which we find as readable today as they were ever intended; particularly when we find items like this;

Dr Jortin wrote a Latin epitaph on a favourite cat. Translated, it reads;

Worn out with age and dire disease, a cat,
Friendly to all, save wicked mouse and rat:
I'm sent at last to ford the Stygian lake,
And to the infernal coast a voyage make.
Me PROSERPINE receiv'd, and smiling said,
"Be bless'd within these mansions of the dead
Enjoy among thy velvet-footed loves,
Elysium's sunny banks and shady groves."
"But if I've well deserv'd, (O gracious Queen,)
If patient under sufferings I have been,
Grant me at at least one night to visit home again
Once more to see my home, and mistress dear,
And purr these grateful accents in her ear.
Thy faithful cat, thy poor departed slave.
Still loves her mistress e'en beyond the grave."

As an island race we have, perhaps, been insulated against attitudes that, abroad, have formed part of other peoples' culture for centuries. Cat worship, on Corpus Christi Day - June 2nd, may be virtually unknown to many in Britain nowadays but in the Middle Ages, animals formed as prominent a part in the worship of the time as they had done in the old religion of Egypt.

The cat was a very important personage in religious festivals at Aix, in Provence. On the festival of Corpus Christi, the finest Tom cat in the country, wrapt in swaddling clothes like a child, was exhibited in a magnificent shrine to public admiration. Every knee was bent, every hand strewed flowers or poured incense, and 'Grimalkin' was treated in all respects as the god of the day.

However, on the Festival of St John, a couple of weeks later, poor Tom's fate was unpleasantly reversed. A number of the tabby tribe were put into a wicker basket and thrown alive into the midst of an immense fire, kindled in the public square by the bishop and his clergy.

Hymns and anthems were sung, and processions were made by the priests and people in honour of the sacrifice.

The pagan Egyptians on the other hand held cats in high esteem and considered the form of a cat symbolised the moon, or Isis, and placed it upon their systrum, an instrument of religious worship and divination. Wild cats were kept by our ancient pagan ancestors for hunting. The officers who had charge of these cats seem to have held appointments of equal consequence with the masters of the king's hounds; they were called 'catatores.'"

In the old Welsh laws, a kitten from its birth till it could see was valued at a penny; when it began to mouse at twopence; and after it had killed mice at fourpence, which was the price of a calf. Cats neither like to be put out of their way, nor to be kept out of their food and, turning our attention to more recent religions again our friend from the past, William Hone, provides this story;

"In cloisters wherein people are immured in catholic countries, to keep or make them of that religion, it is customary to announce the hours of meals by ringing a bell. In a cloisters in France, a cat that was kept there was used never to receive any victuals till the bell rung, and she therefore never failed to be within hearing of it.

One day, however, she happened to be shut up in a solitary apartment, and the bell rang in vain, as far as regarded her. Being some hours after liberated from her confinement, she ran, half famished, to the place where a plate of victuals used generally to be set for her, but found none this time. In the afternoon the bell was heard ringing at an unusual hour, and when the people of the cloisters came to see what was the cause of it, they found the cat hanging upon the bell-rope, and setting it in motion as well as she was able, in order that she might have her dinner served up to her."

There is also a surprising instance of the sensibility of cats recorded by William Hone;

"In the year 1783, two cats belonging to a merchant in Messina, in Sicily, announced to him the approach of an earthquake. Before the first shock was felt, these two animals seemed anxiously to endeavour to work their way through the floor of the room in which they were.

Their master observing their fruitless efforts, opened the door for them. At a second and third door, which they likewise found shut, they repeated their efforts, and on being set completely at liberty, they ran straight through the streets, and out of the gate of the town. The merchant, whose curiosity was excited by this strange conduct of the cats, followed them into the fields, where he again saw them scratching and burrowing in the earth. Soon after there was a violent shock of an earthquake, and many of the houses in the city fell down, of which the merchant's was one, so that he indebted for his life to the singular foreboding of his cats."

An Arab verse of note reminds us that we should look to ourselves;

A man of kindness to an animal is kind, but brutal actions show a brutal mind.
Remember, Did He who made thee, also make a brute,
He who gave thee speech and reason, formed many an animal mute.
They can't complain; But God's all-seeing eyes, Behold thy cruelty, He hears their cries.

They were designed thy servants, not thy drudge.
Remember ! Their creator is thy Judge.

Personal translation.

The words of two friends we have, next, put side by side, with reason, since one provides us with a measure of pleasure at what they have, while the other reminds of the pleasures we might provide.

A Dog's Life
Black satin rippling in the sun,
Your tail a white tipped banner,
Wet snuffling nose contacting earth,
In such a questing manner.

Four twinkling feet in spotless socks,
Two brown eyes mutely trusting,
Ears lifted to the slightest sound,
Pink velvet tongue a thrusting.

Joy of the chase, when veiled by spray,
To set smug sea-gulls flocking,
Swift footed hare bursts from the grass,
Her speed your stride is mocking.

A friendly voice, a plate of food,
A bed, are all dogs ask for,
Which knows the way to happiness.
The canine, or the master?

Lament of the Oldest Inhabitant
I've waited many months to see
If somebody will care for me;
The problem is I'm getting on
And all my energy has gone.

Muzzle grey, and slow of pace
>I can't compete as they all race
>To greet each one who wants a pet;
>I'm old, and slow and grey, and yet
>If somebody wanted me
>I'd give them all my loyalty

I had a home in days gone by -
>My owner died, so here I lie....
>I'm waiting patiently to see
>If somebody will care for me.

Consider now these words, on rats and mice, and cats;
>"Ye rats, in triumph elevate your ears !
>Exult, ye mice ! for fate's abhorred shears
>Of Dick's nine lives have slit the cat-gut nine;
>Henceforth he mews midst choirs of cats divine !"

In our television world, with instant access provided for us to entertainment, of a sort some would say, the art of theatre actor has been completely lost to all who stir not from the settee. It has also been lost to many who pay to see their favourite Tv star struggle to project their lines beyond the first few rows of the stalls.

In the 19th century a singer referred to by name, politely and correctly as times required, as Mr Huddesford, was popular for his *Monody on the Death of Dick, an Academical Cat* and its very words indicate that it could not have been performed 'quietly' except in parts where the actor and singer used his art to the full, and dared his audience draw breath lest they should miss a word.

The 'lives' of the Academical Cat, most recently named Dick, are traced by the singer from the Flood, to the recent, Victorian, time of Dick's recent demise; since Dick is finally mewing among 'divine choirs.'

In tracing this route across the centuries, Huddesford suggests that Dick was once an associate of Rutterkin, a cat who was "cater-cousin to the great-great-great-great-great-great-great-great-grandmother of Grimalkin, and first cat in the caterie of an old woman who was tried for bewitching a daughter of the Countess of Rutland in the sixteenth century."

The monodist connects him with cats of great renown in the annals of witchcraft; a science whereto they have been allied as closely as poor old women, one of whom, it appears, on the authority of an old pamphlet entitled "*Newes from Scotland,*" &c. printed in the year 1591,

"*confessed that she took a cat and christened it, &c. and that in the night following, the said cat was conveyed into the midst of the sea by all these witches sayling in their RIDDLES or CIVES (seives), and so left the said cat before the towne of Leith in Scotland. This done, there did arise such a tempest at sea as a greater hath not been seen, &c. Againe it is confessed, that the said christened cat was the cause of the kinges majestie's shippe, at his coming forthe of Denmark, had a contrarie winde to the rest of the shippes then being in his companie, which thing was most straunge and true, as the kinges majestie acknowledgeth, for when the rest of the shippes had a fair and good winde, then was the winde contrarie, and altogether against his majestie,*" &c.

All sorts of cats, according to Huddesford, lamented the death of his favourite, whom he calls "premier cat among the catalogue," and who, preferring sprats to all other fish;-

"Had swallow'd down a score without remorse,
And three fat mice slew for a second course,
But, while the third his grinders dyed with gore,
Sudden those grinders clos'd - to grind no more!
And, dire to tell ! commissioned by Old Nick,

A catalepsy made an end of DICK.
Calumnious cats who circulate faux pas,
And reputations maul with murd'rous claw ;
Shrill cats whom fierce domestic brawls delighte,
Cross cats who nothing want but teeth to bite,
Starch cats of puritanic aspect sad,
And learned cats who talk their husbands mad;
Confounded cats who cough, and croak, and cry,
And maudlin cats who drink eternally;
Fastidious cats who pine for costly cates,
And jealous cats who catechise their mates;
Cat-prudes who, when they're asked the question, squall,
And ne'er give answers categorical;
Uncleanly cats, who never pare their nails,
Cat-gossips full of Canterbury tales,
Cat-grandams vex'd with asthmas and catarrhs,
And superstitious cats who curse their stars;
Cats of each class, craft, calling, and degree
Mourn DICK'S calamitous catastrophe!
Yet while I chant the cause of RICHARD'S end,
Ye sympathizing cats, your tears suspend!
Then shed enough to float a dozen whales,
And use, for pocket-handkerchiefs, your tails! -
Ah ! tho' thy bust adorns no sculptur's shrine,
No vase thy relics rare to fame consign,
No rev'rend characters thy rank express,
Nor hail thee, DICK ! D.D. nor F.R.S.
Tho' no funereal cypress shade thy tomb
For thee the wreaths of Paradise shall bloom,
There, while GRIMALKIN'S mew her RICHARD greets
A thousand cats shall purr on purple seats :
E'en now I see, descending from his throne,
Thy venerable cat, O Whittington!
The kindred excellence of RICHARD hail,
And wave with joy his gratulating tail!
There shall the worthies of the whisker'd race
Elysian mice o'er floors of sapphire chase,

Midst beds of aromatic marum stray,
Or raptur'd rove beside the Milky Way.
Kittens, than eastern hour is fairer seen,
Whose bright eyes glisten with immortal green,
Shall smooth for tabby swains their yielding fur,
And to their amorous mews assenting purr.-
There, like Alcmena's shall GRIMALKIN'S SON
In bliss repose, - his mousin' labours done,
Fate, envy, curs, time, tide, and traps defy,
And caterwaul to all eternity."

Actors can change the mood of an audience in an instant and the work of some of our friends achieve the same effect. We learned from one of the Vicar's Dog;

"A funeral was in progress, and as the coffin proceeded up the aisle the vicar's little black and white spaniel, not noted for quiet behaviour, entered the church, trotted up to the coffin, sniffed and then walked back down the aisle and out of the church.

The vicar's wife, who was in the congregation apologised afterwards to the widow, who said, "Oh, didn't you know, my husband was a vet, he'd have been delighted!"

Burges Johnson tickled our fancy with

Tickle Me, Please
I like the way the world is made
(Tickle me, please, behind the ears)
With part in the sun and part in the shade
(Tickle me, please, behind the ears)
This comfortable spot beneath a tree
Was probably planned for you and me;
Why do you suppose God made a flea?
Tickle me more behind the ears.

Pleasure was also the theme of ;

Hold That Tiger
All thoughts of mouse safaris,   And tiger hunts have fled
Pampered puss is home again,   Asleep upon the bed!

J. A. B who lives near our Devon friend, Elizabeth Hampton, provided her with a fragmentary but delightful little poem he had read, and loved, and we were pleased that, because of them both, we can all share it;

Master, behold thy servant, he is rising 3 months old.
He is mostly head and tummy & his legs are uncontrolled,
But in thy certain wisdom, thou took him on thy knee,
Master, art thou pleased with him?
He's very pleased with thee!

Similarly, another we are pleased to share will undoubtedly remind other owners of pet/person relationships present or past;

My Cat
Majestic stance, familiar glance,
Soft fur and velvet paws,
Climbing a tree or curled on your knee,
Watch out for those hidden claws.

Stalking at night, hidden from sight,
Listening to nocturnal sound
A creature of mood, but the hour for food,
Will always find you around.

With nimble feet, mischievous, sweet,
Chasing a mouse or a gnat,
You hate the wet, and trips to the vet,
My own peculiar cat.

176

You groom with care, (disturb if you dare)
Fastidious, cunning and smart,
A curious blend, but my dear little friend,
For you there's a place in my heart.

The pet/person relationship was one explored to the full by writers in the past, and the actors who performed these works to audiences that continually wanted more. Prometheus Percival Pipps was one such writer who told, with no added pun intended, many a sad tale that provided an actor with a living for a long long time;

My friends they are cutting me, one and all
With a changed and a cloudy brow;
But my little dog always would come at my call
And why has he not come now?

Oh! If he be living, he'd greet me, - but why
Do I hope with a doubtful "If?"
When I come, and there is not a joy in his eye-
When I come, and his tail lieth stiff?

Ah me ! Not a single friend may I keep! -
From the false I am gladly free,
And the true and the trusty have fallen asleep,
And sleep - without dreaming of me!

I have got my own soul fastened firmly and tight,
And my cold heart is safe in bosom; -
But I would not trust 'em out of my sight -
Or I'm positive I should lose 'em!

My one sole comrade is now no more!
And I needs must mumble and mutter,
That he, who lived in a kennel before,
At last should die in a gutter!

He could fight any beast from a cow to a rat,
And catch any bird for his feast:
But, ah ! he was killed by a big brick-bat
And a bat's not a bird nor a beast!

He died of a blow! - 't was a sad hard blow
Both to me and the poor receiver;
I wish that instead 'twere a fever, I know; -
For his bark might have cured a fever!

His spirit, escaped from his carnal rags,
Is a poodle all wan and pale;
It howls an inaudible howl,- and it wags
The ghost of a shadowy tail!

Old Charon will tout for his penny in vain,
If my Bob but remembers his tricks;
For he, who often sprang over my cane,
Will easily leap over the Styx!

If Cerberus snarls at the gently dead,
He'll act but a dogged part:
The fellow may, perhaps, have a treble head,
But he'll have but a base bad heart!

Farewell my dear Bib, I will keep your skin,
And your tail with its noble tuft;
I have kept it through life, rather skinny and
thin, -
Now I will have it properly stuff'd.

While the theatre audience enjoyed a 'performance' often, a
few words can convey a great deal;

"Money will buy you a fine dog, but only love can make him
wag his tail."

"A well trained dog will make no attempt to share your lunch.
He will just make you
feel too guilty to enjoy it."

"A dog believes you are what you think you are."

"My dog can hear the rustle of a chocolate wrapper from a
distance of 100 yards. So why can't he hear me bawling his
name from ten feet when I want him to come to me?"

"The most affectionate creature in the world - is a wet dog."

A Dog's Prayer
A master or a mistress kind
Who understands a doggie mind
A 'walkie' and a meal a day
That's all I ask for when I pray

Found as a tiny, abandoned pup by a policeman, adopted by
SB, and appropriately named Bobby, SB wrote this sad
dedication when her friend died, at the age of nine. Her words
will echo the thoughts of many who would only change a
name:

Remembrance
No-one to greet me when I rise
No-one to stare with appealing brown eyes,
Now days are lonely, and hills are steep,
Bobby, my Bobby has fallen asleep.
The love that he gave me brought joy untold,
My dear little friend didn't live to grow old.
See you later.

A friend, JCD, very recently passed the comment, 'we are
creating our tomorrow's, today' and while we were
researching parts of this chapter we found some poems by
Ralph Hodgson, who was born over 125 years ago, in 1872.

His poems drew attention to problems that we can still identify with today. Some of the animals he refers to have benefited from people like him creating their 'tomorrows' in their own day. Others have yet to do so, more could added to his list, and our tomorrows await our attention;

The Bells of Heaven
'Twould ring the bells of Heaven
The wildest peal for years
If Parson lost his senses
And people came to theirs,
And he and they together
Knelt down with angry prayers
For tamed and shabby tigers,
And dancing dogs and bears,
And wretched, blind pit ponies,
And little hunted hares.

Ending this section on a theatrical note proved no difficulty whatsoever, and in the modern manner of taking something from past and revising it for the present we can do no better than share a poem we have particularly enjoyed.

It was drawn to our attention by a friend who was certain that we would appreciate some verses written by a well known puss;

IF   by Rudyard Kipling's Cat
If you can disappear when all about you
Are madly searching for you everywhere,
And then just when they start to leave without you,
Turn up as if you always were right there;

If you can shed your hair in any season
And cough up half of all that you devour,
And rush from room to room without a reason
Then sit and stare at nothing for an hour;

If you can kill the baby birds that twitter,
But not the voles that eat bulbs by the score;
If you can scatter heaps of kitty litter,
Yet still leave droppings strewn across the floor;

If you can tear a precious rug to tatters,
But keep your scratching post unmarked by claw;
If you can play with china till it shatters,
But never touch your cat toys with a paw;

If you can try to nap where someone's sitting,
Although there is another empty chair,
Then rub against his ankle without quitting
Until he rises from your favourite lair;

If you can whine and whimper by a portal
Until the bolted door is opened wide,
Then howl as if you've got a wound that's mortal
Until he comes and lets you back inside;

If you can give a guest a nasty spiking,
But purr when you are petted by a thief,
If you can find the food not to your liking
Because they put some cheese in with the beef;

If you can leave no proffered hand unbitten,
And pay no heed to any rule or ban,
Then all will say you are a Cat, my kitten,
And - which is more - you'll make a fool of Man!

Chapter 10

Angels Don't Cry - Do They?

On Wednesday, January 14th, 1998, page 5 of the Daily Mail, one of Britain's most popular newspapers was given over to an article under the headline "The Grunt Escape" and a reporter provided details of a duo that were to capture the nation's attention in a spectacular manner. "On the run, pigs who saved themselves from getting the pork chop" began the enthusiastic 'reporter' who then proceeded to give his, or her, readers the facts.

Weighing in at 110lbs, a couple of Ginger Tamworth boars had been in line for the abattoir on market day at Malmesbury, in Wiltshire, on the previous Thursday but had escaped after a fellow pig had been led off to its fate. The determined duo had apparently run rings around slaughterhouse men in the abattoir yard before finding a hole in the fence, and departing without further delay.

The runaway pigs were by now enjoying their sixth day of freedom, and became media celebrities as Butch and Sundance, The Tamworth Two.

Television news programmes, radio, and the newspapers, carried a constant stream of information on the escapees who had swum the River Avon in the bid for freedom. The nation watched and waited as trappers, camera teams, reporters and photographers followed every sighted trotter print.

With a death penalty hanging over them Butch and Sundance, hogged the headlines and probably commanded as much if not more TV and radio news-time and column inches in the press than any human parading and posturing in the political, sporting, or entertainment arenas at the time.

Animal behaviour experts advised people that the elusive pair would be drawing on the natural cunning and survival instinct of their breed to avoid capture.

An animal psychologist was interviewed who helped allay growing fears for the pigs' safety by confirming that the couple would have no problems coping in the wild. Explaining that pigs were versatile and intelligent animals, the psychologist suggested that the trauma of their journey to the abattoir had probably caused the pigs to bolt for freedom. The conclusion drawn was that the Tamworth Two must have experienced something unpleasant, saw the opportunity to escape, and had taken it.

The future interests of the Butch and Sundance were taken up the Daily Mail which appealed to readers to 'Help To Save Their Bacon.' Televisions' popular 'Animal Hospital' presenter, Rolf Harris added his backing to the newspaper's initiative, and potential providers of sanctuary for the pigs appeared.

On Saturday, 17th January, the Daily Mail was advising the nation of its part in rescuing Butch from the wild, confirming that only hours later Sundance had come in from the cold, and that the perky pair were now set to live their future lives, 'high on the hog.' Television coverage of the great escape had been beamed across Europe, America, and Asia. At the height of interest in the story of the Tamworth Two it was estimated that 150 photographers and camera crews had been trotting around Malmsbury and the wilds of Wiltshire snapping up every tit-bit of information they could find.

Poking through the pedigree of the pigs, a reporter revealed that the pair were not pure Tamworths at all and while their mother, who came from Dorset, had been of that breed, their father was a boar called Amadeus. This couple met, briefly, at Bolehyde Manor, the Wiltshire residence of Lord Cairns, the former home of the Camilla Parker Bowles family.

The Vegetarian Society reported that the adventures of Butch and Sundance had started a wave of interest in vegetarianism and that it was receiving three times its normal number of phone calls daily. The British Pig Association, however, did not foresee a reduction in the popularity of pork among the population despite the national concern expressed for the Tamworth Two. One of Britain's biggest toy manufacturers responded to the public demand for Butch and Sundance to be immortalized by hastening to produce souvenir pigs in time to trot them out at the forthcoming International Toy and Hobby Fair. As the British aircraft carrier *HMS Invincible* headed through the Suez Canal to the Gulf to reinforce the powerful US military presence there, in a show of support to the Americans over Iraq, Butch and Sundance were on their way home.

While the warnings from London and Washington to Saddam Hussein were ones of possible military action against him, little more than a week after they were catapulted into the world's spotlight, the Tamworth Two were settling down to their own less threatened future. Their exploits were no longer headline news, but they have not been forgotten. Occasionally the newspapers publish a brief comment about their progress through retirement.

During their period of fame, many thousands of words must have been written about Butch and Sundance. Theirs was a story that captured the nation, and much of the world. It was decidedly different, exciting, inspirational, heartwarming, and had a happy ending.

When our friend Ray Branch, kindly sent us some material which he said we could including in our work, not being ones to accept co-incidence, we knew that there was a sentence or comment somewhere in our Tamworth Two files that were relevant. Did the pigs have message for us all?

From the Harry Edwards Spiritual Healing Sanctuary, near Guildford, England, Ray Branch sent us some back copies of the centre's magazine and also added a few photocopies of items he thought might interest us, particularly. One of them seemed to leap out of the envelope. It was an article titled 'How Animals Can Die,' and had been written by the late Harry Edwards.

"Like humans, animals possess the qualities of love, and enjoyment of association one with another; they are appreciative of the sense of security that human care gives them, and readily sense friendliness and affection.

The primitive feelings of terror and fear are easily aroused, and because their faculties of perception and appreciation of consequences are limited, they quickly surrender to panic and terror. Animals sense brutal intentions as truly they are sensible to friendly ones.

Generally, an animal's fear is far more intense than that of a human being because it does not possess a reasoning mind, nor can it look ahead from the immediate present. Its mind becomes panic-stricken and seeks its physical escape, often hurting itself in the process. If the act of ending an animal's life is quick, and it is not associated with brutality and atmospheres such as those in a slaughterhouse, then the act of leaving the physical life need not cause suffering.

When, however, animals are taken from their home surroundings to be slaughtered, they become apprehensive, and fearful of that which is before them, and when in strange hands, devoid of love, treated roughly if not brutally, their fears increase and turn to terror-stricken panic. On reaching the place of slaughter their sufferings reach a crescendo in sensing the intention that they are going to be killed.

When animals are caused continual hurt and suffer agonies of pain for a period of time before they die, as in animal experimentation, the quality of fear and suffering is more deeply seated, so that when they arrive into spirit life they continue to hold in the consciousness the memories of their sufferings.

Because animals do not possess the reasoning faculty to a marked degree to appreciate new conditions, and having a more primitive nature, they will retain the fears until they are soothed and they know that they are not in peril any longer. An animal can endure pain and yet be free from terror, but when it is forced to experience both pain and terror, as that associated with vivisection and the slaughter-house, then it arrives in spirit life in a distressful state. It may not be fully understood that humans who become accustomed to causing suffering to animals with cruelties and killings, also suffer much in spirit life, as they become conscious of the evil they have done.

On arrival in spirit life, animals continue to be fearful because they retain the memory of their earthly experiences, but then they receive nursing and soothing until the fears are overcome and serenity returns. It will be a happy day when mankind realizes that animals - like themselves - possess qualities of love and appreciation of kindliness as well as those of mental fear and suffering, and have a right to a happy life with opportunities to fulfil its purpose, after which there should be a period of restfulness in retirement.

Surely this is the way of life that God intended for all living creations, and if this could be so, then they would arrive in spirit life peacefully and free from anguish.

Among the thousands of words written about the Tamworth Two were the comments of a psychologist; remember them? The psychologist had suggested that; 'the trauma of their journey to the abattoir had probably caused the pigs to bolt for freedom. The conclusion drawn was that the Tamworth Two must have experienced something unpleasant, saw the opportunity to escape, and had taken it'. The psychologist had been explaining that pigs were versatile and intelligent animals; are we any less versatile or less intelligent an animal?

Who was St Richard of Chichester really speaking to when addressed animals bound for slaughter;

"Poor innocent little creatures; if you were reasoning beings and could speak you would curse us. For we are the cause of your death, and what have you done to deserve it?"

We are quite used to receiving calls and letters from friends who are, often it seems, in need of guidance. While all that we can do is to offer to share our experiences with them, we have perhaps been fortunate in being also able to add the experiences that others share with us. Invariably, amongst it all, a piece of information, a phrase, a sentence or two, seems to supply an answer, and we remain just a channel.

LZR made contact with us from the USA, through a Caribbean friend, in January 1999. On a 'what do you make of this' basis, she was in need of some information regarding a ghost cat that was in her apartment.

"Cats love me. They walk up to me all the time and they jump in my lap. I love cats, but I am very allergic to them so I never make contact with them unless they happen to jump in my lap. Still, over the past 40 years I have cared for several cats that my children brought home. None of these animals are still alive or in my life. I've moved around the USA a great deal and since I can't keep an animal indoors, I have no pets.

When I moved into my latest apartment almost a year ago, a Wiccan friend said, "There was a cat in this apartment before you." I told her I didn't think so because my allergies are so bad that I would have had a reaction if there HAD been a pet in the apartment, and management said that it was a "pet free" apartment. Then last month, just around Christmas time, I saw a ghost cat running about the place. It is friendly to me but, so far, I have been the only person to have seen it. However, my canary goes crazy at times flying about his cage and acting like something is tormenting him. Sometimes the bird lets out a distress cry. Also, ornaments fell off the tree, and pieces of my créche got knocked over.

Are these ghost cats good or will it make mischief? I don't mind it being around if it doesn't do any harm. What is your experience with them and why did it choose now to make itself known almost a year later?

It isn't often that we come across pets that have crossed the Rainbow Bridge and then 'adopt' a friend but we have many friends whose pet/companion has crossed the bridge but whose boisterous spirit needs a little calming influence. Put two and two together and it will always make four but even LZR was adrift in suggesting that she had been the only one to have seen the ghost cat. Alright, she did actually say that she'd been the only 'person' to see the cat but we should never ignore what our pet/companions have say to us.

Our e-mail friend, FMA, has a father on whom she could rely for an opinion.

"My father became very bonded with our Siamese cat, Victoria. After she crossed over the Rainbow Bridge, my father insisted that she would come and sleep with him at night; he would feel her jump up on the bed and walk around. This is surprising, since my father is the last person you would think would believe in anything paranormal. But knowing Victoria, it is undoubtedly so; she loved him very much and probably didn't want to leave him. I had a cat who had a large tumor. The vet said there was no cure, but as long as she seemed happy to let her be. She seemed pretty well off until one day I came home from work, and she was hiding under a chair upstairs. Then she came downstairs and fell over; she couldn't get up.

I called the vet and made arrangements for her to be put to sleep. After I had done it, I felt very guilty and anxious; had I rushed it? Maybe she should have had more time.

One night, I had a dream where I heard her little meow and felt her crawl on any lap and start to purr. I woke up suddenly - it had seemed very real. Then I knew that she had really visited me! She had set my mind at ease that she was happy and that I had done the right thing and that she still loved me."

When her father found that his bond with Victoria was unbroken, the knowledge must have provided him with comfort. Just knowing of the peace of mind that Frances herself gained from her cat's visit, when she still felt guilty about her own actions, might help others who know all too well what that guilt feels like. It is not only items about pets from the other side that we find inspirational though.

Thanks to our good friend Elizabeth who lives in Devon, England, we have been able to share the experiences of some of her friends, and their ways of drawing attention to a pertinent point or two, including The Last Will and Testament of 'Agnes' - written by Agnes's master which makes not only entertaining reading but also provides guidance.

"My material possessions are few and I leave them all to you. A collar chewed on one end, with two studs missing, a lumpy dog bed, and my chipped water dish. I leave you half a rubber ball which you will find under the refrigerator, a rubber mouse with the whistle missing, located behind the kitchen stove, and dozens of bones under the rose bushes and flower beds. Mostly I leave you memories which are many.

I leave you memories of soft brown eyes, and a stubby tail, a brown flecked nose and my whine at the back door. I leave you the spot of sunshine that was cast through the window on to the living room rug at 4 o'clock winter afternoons, which I appropriated for my own as I curled into a ball. I leave you a tattered rug in front of your easy chair, which was not repaired with exactly the same kind of yarn. I chewed it when I was a senseless five-month puppy.... remember?

I also leave you the memory of my first spanking and my forgiveness. I leave you a hollow trench which you will find under the bushes near the front porch, where I found asylum during the hot summer days. It's full of leaves now so you might have trouble finding it. I bequeath you the sound I made scampering through a carpet of October leaves when we tramped through the woods together.

I leave you remembered moments of mornings sitting together on the bank awaiting that first nibble. I remember your laughter at my first encounter with the rabbit I couldn't catch. I leave you my devotion, my sympathy when things go wrong, my bark when you raise your voice in needless anger, and my frustration when I curl my tail underneath me when you scold me.

I never went to church and I never heard a sermon. Yet without ever having spoken a word in my life, I leave you lessons in patience, tolerance, love and understanding."

The connection between our two pigs and the stories of ghost cats, contented cats, and a dog that put people in their place in his 'will' may not be clear, yet. However, in each situation, as with most we have so far shared, intentions mean more than might be apparent.

One Friday in November 1998 our American friend, MBG, was prompted to share some of the experiences she'd had involving cats, with us. Her experiences began with her Burmese mix, Kokomo, who had been owned previously by her eldest sister but, when elder sister moved to Florida, Kokomo stayed with the family, and he and MBG became quite attached.

"He was very lovable and never meowed. I was told by the vet that it was a, low meow. Kokomo was just under two years old when a neighbor who lived on the next block stuck fly tape on him while we were gone.

We tried real hard to get the sticky stuff

off to no avail. He eventually ate it off and I knew he shouldn't have been doing that, but I was 12 years old at the time and never thought anything of it. Not too long after that, he meowed. It was the first time I ever heard a sound come out of him. I knew then that he was real sick and we had also noticed that he had trouble urinating. Mom pushed on his bladder and he let out the most awful noise. It was unbearable.

We brought him to the vet and all he did was clear the passageway. The cat had bladder stones. I knew that he had to have surgery but the vet never even mentioned it. He said that Koko would be fine. Well, he wasn't.

When it had to be done again we were going out of town and wouldn't be back until late so we left him there. Somehow I knew that was the last time I would ever see him.

We came to pick him up the next day and the secretary told us that he had died. It was heartbreaking news, he was the first cat that I had. He died July 27, 1991 at only one and a half years old.

About a month later, I was watching TV and wished that he was there. I glanced sideways and I could have sworn that he was right there. I looked again and he was gone. I don't know if that was just my imagination or if he was really there. After that, it was easier for me to go on. I shed a tear every once in awhile (like when I was typing this story), but it doesn't happen that often.

My other story is about my tabby Ernie who I had gotten after Kokomo died.

He was the greatest cat that I ever had. He always slept by my side at night and made me feel better when I was sad. He lived for 3 years. Ernie was always determined to get outside and it eventually got the better of him. He also developed bladder *stones but I didn't know that until the night he died.*

Ernie had disappeared for 2 days and I think he was in the house the entire time because I heard a thump upstairs and there he was. I noticed that he couldn't walk very well so I brought him upstairs and laid him on my bed. I could see that he was in a lot of pain.

Ernie's death was more painful for me because I watched him die. He tried to fight it with everything he had. I watched his breathing slow down and then when I laid my hand on his side he would breathe faster. Have you ever seen an animal die? They lurch and gag, it was awful. I would have given anything to end his suffering.

I didn't even think of calling a vet to come put him down. I guess a part of me wished that he was just sick and would be fine in the morning. The only real part that I regret is falling asleep on him. I wished I could have stayed up to say good-bye. I woke up about two hours later and he was gone. I think his death will bother me for the rest of my life.

Ernie was meant to be in my life. He was born on my birthday (his brothers and sisters were born after midnight), so I guess that may be why we connected. His mother belonged to a friend of mine and she always had the same coloured kittens. Ernie was different because he always followed me, and no one else. I guess he chose me to be with him. That's not the only thing though that makes this strange.

About a year later (after having another cat who got hit by a car when he was 9 months old), I happened onto another tabby kitten that looked just like Ernie. That's his name too and I'll be danged if Ernie 1 had never died. He is just like him in every way, except that he's not a cuddler (only rarely he is). Ernie 2 is three years old now and I'm afraid that I might lose him. He developed bladder stones once but we caught it in the very first stage so he won't get it anymore. He is on a cat food that helps his urinary tract. But of course he's a roamer and I am trying real hard to keep him inside but it is very difficult.

If Ernie dies soon there will be no more cats for a long time unless he calls to me again. Well I hope these help you a little more, I know I believe in it. Both cats showed me that it can happen and I wish more people would believe in it too."

KFN lives in Norway, and made contact with us after reading the article about "ghostly" pets in the *Your Cat* magazine. He regretted, he said, that he was not being able to contribute any animal ghost story from his own experience but was writing to draw our attention to two books that he thought might be of interest to us in our work.

They were, but instead of including our own thoughts on them here, we will share KFN's own impressions of the works. It was his words that took us a step forward; he has been the one fortunate enough to meet one of the authors and, acting as a channel suits us.

"Stephen Turoff, the famous psychic surgeon, wrote a book called "Seven Steps to Eternity", based on the story of a young, deceased soldier who appeared to him regularly over a period of a couple of years. The soldier, James Leggett, fell in the battle of Somme in the First World War and in the book he tells his story chronologically (which makes it easy to read but means one should read it at least twice to get the whole picture). It is a fascinating account, told with warmth, compassion and humour.

The young Jim was, or is, (Turoff still sees him from time to time) obviously an inquisitive person and he wanted to find out what happens to animals when they die. It would seem that their souls, like ours, return to their "mother soul", carrying with them all their experiences, thus in the long run

194

influencing the behaviour pattern (instincts) of the species. However, unlike ours, their souls do not usually live on. If they do, it is only because of human love and it is not forever.

Judging from the book, animals can survive with us only in heaven, but the second account (see below) and the stories cited from your research suggest that in some instances they may stay with us here on earth, too, even if only for a short time.

When I met Turoff a few weeks ago we spoke about a friend of my mother-in-laws who had drowned trying to save her daughter's dog (which survived). All the thanks she got was that her daughter promptly had her two cats put to sleep. Turoff said he was sure that she would not have allowed her cats to pass over, i.e. they would surely be with her now.

It would seem from "Seven Steps to Eternity" that also your relatives can do this for you. Maybe they or some guardian angel were at work in the following story, which also concerns a soldier.

The second book, "You cannot die" by Ian Currie, contains a lot of information that seems to fit in with Turoff's book although it differs in several key respects and Currie's book seems almost irreligious compared to the deeply Christian spirit of "Seven Steps to Eternity". Currie's story of the homecoming soldier's brief encounter with the recently deceased dog is particularly touching. If it was arranged thus to comfort either him or the dog (or both of them) we shall probably never know, this side of the grave. Neither shall we know who was responsible.

The second story from "You cannot die", of a crippled cat returning to haunt its old territory (where it had also been buried) is strange. James Leggett tells how outside every slaughterhouse there are Keepers of the Light helping the souls of the slaughtered animals to enter the path back to their mother soul. Maybe sometimes animals, like human beings, can get "trapped", not being able to pass on, if they die under distressing circumstances and that this chat revenant needed (and probably finally got from some kindly spirit) help to pass on.

That animals are affected by good spirits is something of which I am absolutely certain. Thousands of people have had their lives touched and blessed by animals in times of extreme emotional crisis. As somebody once said, coincidences happen when God wants to remain anonymous. When my wife and I first met our cat it immediately decided that it wanted to stay with us (it had been looking for a new home for some time but even so ...). I am positive that this thought was planted into its head. I am equally certain that it saved our marriage.

A cat-loving colleague once came home to find a cat on her doorstep. She opened the door for it but it tried to enter through the opening on the hinged side. It turned out that it was blind and just followed the slight draft from the resulting crack. In fact, it was in a very bad way (traffic accident?) with half a leg missing and smelling terribly. It was unable to eat and it could not walk in a straight line but just went around in circles. My colleague took it to the vet and had it put to sleep. How could it have climbed the stairs, being blind and walking around in circles?

What an incredible co-incidence that it came to her, maybe the only one in the whole street who would have helped it. To me the answer is self-evident. My life has taught me again and again not to believe in co-incidences."

We share his views about co-incidences and while our Norwegian friend may not have been able to add any personal 'ghostly' experiences to our files, we have little doubt that his comments will be valued by others and that the matters he has touched upon will be recognised as beacons along the route we have taken since first meeting the Tamworth Two.

Our friends, who are particularly concerned about animals being used for food, may gain some comfort from James Leggett's work. Similarly, the words of Harry Edwards will surely be of help, guidance and comfort to them; but not only to them, we believe.

So many times we hear that the pet/person relationship brings so much joy, but that the parting is filled with sorrow. How can we kill a friend, is the heart breaking question raised in so many ways by many people. How can we ignore a friend in need, is too easy a reply.

Harry Edwards knew that not everyone shared his beliefs, and the guidance he gave didn't demand that they should. His words that,

"Animals sense brutal intentions as truly. If the act of ending an animal's life is quick, and it is not associated with brutality and atmospheres such as those in a slaughterhouse, then the act of leaving the physical life need not cause suffering.,"

are not by co-incidence directed in different directions.

While advising us of our animal friends' recognition of brutality, in all forms, in one direction, he is also advising us that they recognize and understand friendly and loving intentions, in another. How then, can we kill a friend?

Not easily, that is quite certain, and loving intentions do not ease the heartbreak.

We are well aware that our pet/companions understand our friendly intentions at the best of times, when sharing the physical pleasures of a walk a run, a rest, and every other valued fun-filled moment with us. It becomes undeniable then that such understanding exists throughout life, to its very end, at least. Is there not comfort then in understanding that our pet/companions sense our good intentions, even as we end their lives?

"If the act of ending an animal's life is quick, and it is not associated with brutality and atmospheres such as those in a slaughterhouse, then the act of leaving the physical life need not cause suffering."

Perhaps Butch and Sundance were not ready to allow the Keepers of Light to guide their souls but their adventures certainly guided us to pathways new.

We consider ourselves fortunate to have friends who share with us their experiences of devotion, trust, and love, and who recognize that they are indeed in the presence of Angels when they share their lives with their beloved pet/companions. There is much for us all to learn, and of this we are sure.

To gain further understanding it is necessary for us to continue with open minds, to look and be prepared to really see, to listen, and to be silent often enough to allow the wisdom contained in the hearts of others, to be heard.

> All in the April morning,
>   April airs were abroad;
> The sheep with their little lambs
>   Pass'd me on the road;
>
> The sheep with their little lambs
>   Pass'd me on the road.
>   All in an April evening
>   I thought on the Lamb of God
>
> The lambs were weary, and crying

With a weak human cry,
I thought on the Lamb of God
Going meekly to die.

Up in the blue, blue mountains
Dewy pastures are sweet;
Rest for the little bodies
Rest for the little feet

But for the Lamb of God
Up on the hill-top green,
Only a cross of shame
Two stark crosses between.

All in the April evening
April airs were abroad;
I saw the sheep with their lambs
And thought on the Lamb of God

Katharine Tynan Hinkson 1861 - 1931

FREE DETAILED

CATALOGUE

Capall Bann is owned and run by people actively involved in many of the areas in which we publish. A detailed illustrated catalogue is available on request, SAE or International Postal Coupon appreciated. **Titles can be ordered direct from Capall Bann, post free in the UK** (cheque or PO with order) or from good bookshops and specialist outlets.

Do contact us for details on the latest releases at: **Capall Bann Publishing, Freshfields, Chieveley, Berks, RG20 8TF.** Titles include:

A Breath Behind Time, Terri Hector
Angels and Goddesses - Celtic Christianity & Paganism, M. Howard
Arthur - The Legend Unveiled, C Johnson & E Lung
Astrology The Inner Eye - A Guide in Everyday Language, E Smith
Auguries and Omens - The Magical Lore of Birds, Yvonne Aburrow
Asyniur - Womens Mysteries in the Northern Tradition, S McGrath
Beginnings - Geomancy, Builder's Rites & Electional Astrology in the
    European Tradition, Nigel Pennick
Between Earth and Sky, Julia Day
Book of the Veil , Peter Paddon
Caer Sidhe - Celtic Astrology and Astronomy, Vol 1, Michael Bayley
Caer Sidhe - Celtic Astrology and Astronomy, Vol 2 M Bayley
Call of the Horned Piper, Nigel Jackson
Cat's Company, Ann Walker
Celtic Faery Shamanism, Catrin James
Celtic Faery Shamanism - The Wisdom of the Otherworld, Catrin James
Celtic Lore & Druidic Ritual, Rhiannon Ryall
Celtic Sacrifice - Pre Christian Ritual & Religion, Marion Pearce
Celtic Saints and the Glastonbury Zodiac, Mary Caine
Circle and the Square, Jack Gale
Compleat Vampyre - The Vampyre Shaman, Nigel Jackson
Creating Form From the Mist - The Wisdom of Women in Celtic Myth and
    Culture, Lynne Sinclair-Wood
Crystal Clear - A Guide to Quartz Crystal, Jennifer Dent
Crystal Doorways, Simon & Sue Lilly
Crossing the Borderlines - Guising, Masking & Ritual Animal Disguise in the
    European Tradition, Nigel Pennick
Dragons of the West, Nigel Pennick
Earth Dance - A Year of Pagan Rituals, Jan Brodie
Earth Harmony - Places of Power, Holiness & Healing, Nigel Pennick
Earth Magic, Margaret McArthur
Eildon Tree (The) Romany Language & Lore, Michael Hoadley
Enchanted Forest - The Magical Lore of Trees, Yvonne Aburrow
Eternal Priestess, Sage Weston

Eternally Yours Faithfully, Roy Radford & Evelyn Gregory
Everything You Always Wanted To Know About Your Body, But So Far
    Nobody's Been Able To Tell You, Chris Thomas & D Baker
Face of the Deep - Healing Body & Soul, Penny Allen
Fairies in the Irish Tradition, Molly Gowen
Familiars - Animal Powers of Britain, Anna Franklin
Fool's First Steps, (The) Chris Thomas
Forest Paths - Tree Divination, Brian Harrison, Ill. S. Rouse
From Past to Future Life, Dr Roger Webber
Gardening For Wildlife Ron Wilson
God Year, The, Nigel Pennick & Helen Field
Goddess on the Cross, Dr George Young
Goddess Year, The, Nigel Pennick & Helen Field
Goddesses, Guardians & Groves, Jack Gale
Handbook For Pagan Healers, Liz Joan
Handbook of Fairies, Ronan Coghlan
Healing Book, The, Chris Thomas and Diane Baker
Healing Homes, Jennifer Dent
Healing Journeys, Paul Williamson
Healing Stones, Sue Philips
Herb Craft - Shamanic & Ritual Use of Herbs, Lavender & Franklin
Hidden Heritage - Exploring Ancient Essex, Terry Johnson
Hub of the Wheel, Skytoucher
In Search of Herne the Hunter, Eric Fitch
Inner Celtia, Alan Richardson & David Annwn
Inner Mysteries of the Goths, Nigel Pennick
Inner Space Workbook - Develop Thru Tarot, C Summers & J Vayne
Intuitive Journey, Ann Walker Isis - African Queen, Akkadia Ford
Journey Home, The, Chris Thomas
Kecks, Keddles & Kesh - Celtic Lang & The Cog Almanac, Bayley
Language of the Psycards, Berenice
Legend of Robin Hood, The, Richard Rutherford-Moore
Lid Off the Cauldron, Patricia Crowther
Light From the Shadows - Modern Traditional Witchcraft, Gwyn
Living Tarot, Ann Walker
Lore of the Sacred Horse, Marion Davies
Lost Lands & Sunken Cities (2nd ed.), Nigel Pennick
Magic of Herbs - A Complete Home Herbal, Rhiannon Ryall
Magical Guardians - Exploring the Spirit and Nature of Trees, Philip Heselton
Magical History of the Horse, Janet Farrar & Virginia Russell
Magical Lore of Animals, Yvonne Aburrow
Magical Lore of Cats, Marion Davies
Magical Lore of Herbs, Marion Davies
Magick Without Peers, Ariadne Rainbird & David Rankine
Masks of Misrule - Horned God & His Cult in Europe, Nigel Jackson
Medicine For The Coming Age, Lisa Sand MD

Medium Rare - Reminiscences of a Clairvoyant, Muriel Renard
Menopausal Woman on the Run, Jaki da Costa
Mind Massage - 60 Creative Visualisations, Marlene Maundrill
Mirrors of Magic - Evoking the Spirit of the Dewponds, P Heselton
Moon Mysteries, Jan Brodie
Mysteries of the Runes, Michael Howard
Mystic Life of Animals, Ann Walker
New Celtic Oracle The, Nigel Pennick & Nigel Jackson
Oracle of Geomancy, Nigel Pennick
Pagan Feasts - Seasonal Food for the 8 Festivals, Franklin & Phillips
Patchwork of Magic - Living in a Pagan World, Julia Day
Pathworking - A Practical Book of Guided Meditations, Pete Jennings
Personal Power, Anna Franklin
Pickingill Papers - The Origins of Gardnerian Wicca, Bill Liddell
Pillars of Tubal Cain, Nigel Jackson
Places of Pilgrimage and Healing, Adrian Cooper
Practical Divining, Richard Foord
Practical Meditation, Steve Hounsome
Practical Spirituality, Steve Hounsome
Psychic Self Defence - Real Solutions, Jan Brodie
Real Fairies, David Tame
Reality - How It Works & Why It Mostly Doesn't, Rik Dent
Romany Tapestry, Michael Houghton
Runic Astrology, Nigel Pennick
Sacred Animals, Gordon MacLellan
Sacred Celtic Animals, Marion Davies, Ill. Simon Rouse
Sacred Dorset - On the Path of the Dragon, Peter Knight
Sacred Grove - The Mysteries of the Forest, Yvonne Aburrow
Sacred Geometry, Nigel Pennick
Sacred Nature, Ancient Wisdom & Modern Meanings, A Cooper
Sacred Ring - Pagan Origins of British Folk Festivals, M. Howard
Season of Sorcery - On Becoming a Wisewoman, Poppy Palin
Seasonal Magic - Diary of a Village Witch, Paddy Slade
Secret Places of the Goddess, Philip Heselton
Secret Signs & Sigils, Nigel Pennick
Self Enlightenment, Mayan O'Brien
Spirits of the Air, Jaq D Hawkins
Spirits of the Earth, Jaq D Hawkins
Spirits of the Earth, Jaq D Hawkins
Stony Gaze, Investigating Celtic Heads John Billingsley
Stumbling Through the Undergrowth , Mark Kirwan-Heyhoe
Subterranean Kingdom, The, revised 2nd ed, Nigel Pennick
Symbols of Ancient Gods, Rhiannon Ryall
Talking to the Earth, Gordon MacLellan
Taming the Wolf - Full Moon Meditations, Steve Hounsome
Teachings of the Wisewomen, Rhiannon Ryall

The Other Kingdoms Speak, Helena Hawley
Tree: Essence of Healing, Simon & Sue Lilly
Tree: Essence, Spirit & Teacher, Simon & Sue Lilly
Through the Veil, Peter Paddon
Torch and the Spear, Patrick Regan
Understanding Chaos Magic, Jaq D Hawkins
Vortex - The End of History, Mary Russell
Warp and Weft - In Search of the I-Ching, William de Fancourt
Warriors at the Edge of Time, Jan Fry
Water Witches, Tony Steele
Way of the Magus, Michael Howard
Weaving a Web of Magic, Rhiannon Ryall
West Country Wicca, Rhiannon Ryall
Wildwitch - The Craft of the Natural Psychic, Poppy Palin
Wildwood King , Philip Kane
Witches of Oz, Matthew & Julia Philips
Wondrous Land - The Faery Faith of Ireland by Dr Kay Mullin
Working With the Merlin, Geoff Hughes
Your Talking Pet, Ann Walker

FREE detailed catalogue and FREE 'Inspiration' magazine

Contact: Capall Bann Publishing, Freshfields, Chieveley, Berks, RG20 8TF
website: www.capallbann.co.uk